D0058891

TRUTH SEEKER

A Spiritual Adventure of Love, Loss, and Liberation

Erin Reese

Copyright © Erin Reese, 2021

Published by
TRAVEL AND SOUL MEDIA
travelandsoulmedia.com

ISBN: 978-1-7362861-0-4

Cover design by Kelsey Conroy (San Francisco, CA)
Interior design by Sharon Schanzer (New York, NY)
Photos of Ramesh Balsekar and Erin Reese, Author's Collection
Author photo by Alix Rauh

All rights reserved. No part of this book may be reproduced or transmitted in any form or by any means, electronic or mechanical, including photocopying, recording, or by any information storage and retrieval system without written permission from the author or her agents, except for the inclusion of brief quotations in a review.

Also by Erin Reese

Books

The Adventures of Bindi Girl:
Diving Deep Into the Heart of India

Bindi Girl II:
Surrendering to the Soul of India

Contributions

How I Met Ramesh:
The Way Existence Mysteriously Led Spiritual Seekers
to Ramesh Balsekar

Angel Over My Shoulder:
True Stories of Angelic Encounters

This book is dedicated to
my Teacher, Ramesh Balsekar,
and to the *Satguru* within.

When the student is ready, the teacher appears.
When the student is truly ready, the teacher will disappear.
~ Lao Tzu

Contents

Preface

Truth Seeker tells the story of an existential crisis, the end of seeking, and the willingness to lose everything to find true, lasting freedom. This book also shares the profound, inexpressible grace of encountering one's spiritual teacher, or *guru*.

Just as the Beatles and the Rolling Stones have entire catalogs of albums stretching over decades, exhibiting an expansive range of styles, this book is one important slice of a multifaceted life and part of a larger body of work.

I am aware that this story is filtered through my own cultural upbringing, influencing my personal perception and writing at the time these events occurred. A few dates, details, and names of individuals have been altered to smooth out the flow, yet the story unfolds as it occurred in real time.

Finally, readers may find the included glossary to be a helpful reference in translating unfamiliar words and phrases.

May you find inspiration within.

Erin Reese

High Sierras, Northern California
December 2020

Prologue:
Partner In Time

In April 2007, I crawled back to the United States after my second six-month India journey, chronicled in *The Adventures of Bindi Girl*. My return to the States was rocky: I'd brought a broken heart back with me—the ending of my relationship with my travel partner and lover as well as being torn again from Mother India's bosom before I felt fully ready to part. I'd also brought a vicious batch of parasites back home with me. The summer was about regaining my strength, and after three months, my doctor and natural healer gave me clearance to travel again. I was anxious to return to the Motherland.

I'd found through the few months of vagabonding with my recent ex-boyfriend, Jan, in the jungles of India that I could go deeper into the great unknown with a partner in crime by my side. From January through April 2007, traveling side by side in the most adventurous fashion, Jan had taught me tolerance and showed me what I was really made of. For all my solo courage, I'd probably NOT have lived in the jungle amongst cobras and land crabs if it weren't for my campmate encouraging me. I'd tasted the essence of travel-togetherness, even if we didn't make it as a couple in the end. This time, I craved having a boyfriend by my side from the get-go.

And so, I did what any average San Francisco single would do: I posted a personals ad on Craigslist to find a travel companion for my next soul journey, a "partner-in-time," so to speak. And, lo and behold, that partner, Tim, happened to be online that day and responded.

When I first saw Tim's photo and age, ten years my junior, I said to myself, "No way. He's too young!" But something pulled me closer, imploring me to look again. Destiny had tracked me down. Clearly, this good-looking, all-American, blond-haired and blue-eyed boy and I were meant to team up. For what reason, for what duration, I couldn't know.

I had mixed feelings about the whole thing. To be sure, Tim and I were hot for each other—me in my mid-thirties and Tim at twenty-seven made for a steamy combination. But we had radically different approaches to travel, and to life in general. While I was an off-the-beaten-path, hardcore budget backpacker preferring to hang with hippies and hammocks, Tim was from an upper-class Midwestern background that was more accustomed to living in the lap of luxury. I knew we would have our challenges cut out for us.

Still, despite all our personality differences, Tim had something very special. He *emanated*. A palpable force field of pure energy, of beingness, radiated through his eyes, straight to my core. My stressed-out monkey mind would often stop when we were together. *Ah, so this is silence!* I realized. Through the grace of his own spiritual path, Tim was fully in his heart. Underneath the well-to-do façade, he had something that I lacked. And that something was real, honest-to-goodness PEACE OF MIND. The only thing left that I wanted in the whole wide world.

Tim had also been to India two times prior for short visits, yet he'd never fulfilled his desire of visiting the holy mountain of Arunachala in Tiruvannamalai to pay respect to his *Sadguru*, Ramana Maharshi. Tim was also fully disillusioned with the material world of the West, and he was drawn to me as a muse as much as I was pulled to him.

In August 2007, we were both scheduled to start promising professional contracts in San Francisco. At the eleventh hour, both of us told our respective clients that we were out. We just could not ignore the pull to leave for India—together.

Even more than the call of romance and togetherness, I knew I had to get back to India. Let's be more specific: I didn't want to *exist* anymore. I was completely exhausted by and disgusted with the incessant activity of ego, in myself and in the world.

I was willing to give it all up—everything—to end the existential suffering. The fact that Tim was willing to take off with me made it a bit easier, though I was already struggling with the relationship dynamics and our differences. Deep down, I felt stressed and unhappy together, but I was stressed and unhappy alone, too.

When you're flat-out miserable, you're willing to try anything, and India was the place that offered relief. *Away from all this... I'm ready to die anyway...*

So instead of trying to build a life again back in the Bay Area, I shopped for one-way tickets and dusted off my trusty rucksack. In September 2007, Tim walked away from a career in corporate real estate, packed up his Pacific Heights flat, gave the keys to his SUV to his father, and boarded the plane back to India with me.

PART I
The Student is Ready

"World Traveler, Writer, Mystic and Muse—36"
San Francisco
July 3, 2007

World Traveler, Writer,
Mystic and Muse — 36

Just returned from six months in India, finally landing back in SF — for now. I'm a writer and mystic who practices many arts, including astrology, guitar (learning!), and dance/yoga/singing... Pretty mellow (with the occasional rowdy burst), solid spiritual life, entrepreneur, love to go out and listen to live music — especially in outdoor settings. Movies. Musings. Hugs. Long walks in nature, the park, along the ocean. Fresh air, fresh ideas, and getting fresh from time to time. Would be lovely to share some time and rhyme with a like-minded mind-body-world adventurer. A blend of gypsy and groundedness — how's that for a twist? You get the gist. Enjoy your day, in some large or small way. Now get out and play. I should take my own advice. ;)

Because I included two photographs with the ad—one of me with an elephant, walking along the beach in India; the other of me with a guitar, singing—I received a slew of responses. They ran the gamut of "types." Stockbrokers, hippies, musicians, travelers, guys looking for sex, guys looking for mothers of their children, meditators, and yogis—a whole lotta men! But only one caught my eye. The subject read simply: "Mystic."

"Hi, my name is Tim. I've been to India twice and have been on a spiritual path for a long time. I'm probably too young for you anyway—27—but felt to say hi. P.S. What do you mean by mystic?"

I wrote back to ask for a photo and more description of his spiritual life. It is a rare twenty-seven-year-old male who has been on a spiritual path for a long time, and I wanted to hear more. He sent two pictures that endeared me to him immediately: one of him in Tibet, and the other bowing in greeting before a village woman in Vietnam.

Out of eighty responses to my ad, I chose to meet only one. Tim.

Tim wrote to only one. Me.

After we emailed a few times, the clincher came when he sent his birth data. Astrologer that I am, I immediately plugged his time, date, and place of birth into my software. Voilà. *There is something going on here.* Our charts were like overlays to each other—both with prominent Grand Air Trines. And when I put the two together in a relationship composite chart—*wowee zowee!*—something big was bound to occur. The chart clearly spoke of spiritual missions, including teachers and travels in foreign lands. I was intrigued, to say the least.

My own spiritual travel blog is what won Tim over. Who would have thought that a love story about India, replete with amateur photos and tales of woe and tails of snakes, could be the link between two souls looking to bump into each other? Would our searching souls collide?

A week after corresponding by email and speaking on the phone a few times, we arranged to meet in the foggy Richmond District of San Francisco, where I was staying.

My immediate reaction upon meeting Tim? *The age difference will be impossible to get past. This will never work. I don't want to relive some sort of* How Stella Got Her Groove Back *cougar episode.*

We went for a long walk to a cliffside labyrinth on the crest of the Pacific Ocean near Land's End and Baker Beach. Within ten minutes of our walk, we ran smack dab into a gal I had met last fall in Delhi. A wave of travel synchronicity. *Something is up.*

The chemistry between us was crackling. My head kept telling me, "He's too young!" But my body and my heart were screaming for more, more, more. Sparks were flying.

The next day I decided to drive over to his house to tell him we couldn't see each other. I needed to tell Tim that we were too different in age and it would be better to not get involved at all.

Get that. I drive over to his house to see him, to tell him I can't see him anymore. *Uh-huh.*

Sitting across from Tim on the couch in his upper-crust Pacific Heights apartment, he just looked at me when I delivered the news. The next thing I knew, this beautiful young man was kissing me passionately. It took my breath away. I pulled back, speechless, and looked at him in wonder.

"Don't think," he instructed, staring me directly in the eyes. I obliged, gave in, and next thing I knew, we were stumbling toward the bedroom with clothes flying off as we dove into each other wholeheartedly. It was one of the most passionate "first times" ever. Thrilling. Delicious. Fated, and fateful.

There are a few things a free personal ad service like Craigslist can't manufacture, like astrological compatibility, timing, and the willingness to take a little gamble on the romance roulette.

What do you do when your destiny is looking at you, straight in the face?
Do you wave it away, as chance?
This *could* be your lucky break!
To be sure, doubt and fear are some of the strongest pathogens in our

psyche. I was filled with doubt and fear and knew I'd try to resist this pull of destiny.

I told him that, saying, "Tim, I will try to push you away. Don't let me."

"You ain't gettin' away, baby," Tim said. Confidence is a turn-on if I do say so myself. And besides chemistry, astrology, and synchronicity, another reason I didn't ignore Tim altogether is because of an enticing Tarot reading I had received from a native islander on my last trip to India during a short stopover in Thailand…

The Tarot Man

Gulf of Thailand
October 2006

It was pouring rain. I didn't know that Thailand in October is still in the tail end of monsoon season! Nobody told me there'd be days like these. Strange days indeed.

I had come to the island to have a proper beach holiday before getting to India. *Apparently*, the time to decompress on the islands is *after* wintering in India, not before. But I was itching, bitching, moaning, and complaining my way through this otherwise beautiful Southeast Asian paradise, because my soul only wanted to go home, to go OM.

To assuage my grumpiness, I decided to get a Tarot reading. See what was up.

Sitting up in the sweaty attic of a Thai massage parlor, I met the reader. Toothless, stuttering, yet oddly attractive with a strong, graceful build and long dark hair tied at the nape. He was only about thirty. *Young for a shaman*, I thought. He said his name was Tarot Man.

Tarot Man clearly and empathetically explained that I was to be meeting my soul mate very soon. That he would be younger than me, a white guy.

"White guy?" I asked Tarot Man.

"Yeah, he gonna be a white guy."

The way he said it, he emblazoned a picture of an All-American boy in my mind, someone from the U.S. or Canada.

Tarot Man warned me that I would be tempted to push him away.

"Don't," he said. "This relationship gonna be very good for you."

I sat there and took it all in. I knew he wasn't making this stuff up. An advanced Tarot reader myself, I was eying the very cards Tarot Man had laid out before me.

I fervently took notes. This felt serious. And besides, what a glorious vision—an ideal. *Heck, yeah! I'm going to take that one on!*

I also knew astrologically, with lucky Jupiter transiting my seventh house of partnerships that year, I was destined to learn a thing or three about relationships. And learning while on the road offered a special zest.

Tarot Man also told me I would be famous. And that I would live in New York City again someday. And then we were done.

When Tarot Man gave me his business card at the end of the session, I noticed the name printed on the card was "Tim."

Ready to Die
San Francisco
Summer 2007

The following excerpts are from my journals, beginning just a few days before meeting Tim. While outwardly grateful and open to life's possibili-ties, inwardly I was deeply struggling with an existential suffering that nothing outside of myself seemed to fix...

July 4

Dear God, please guide me through this day. Please speak through me, act through me, live your light through me. Please give me peace and serenity. I'm needing joy and love and comfort in whatever way you would provide. I feel like I need therapy. Do I need therapy? Counseling? And by whom? Please guide me. Please inspire me. Please help me.

July 6

So I've been communicating with this guy Tim and I feel he is an in-teresting—young—soul.

July 7

Tim says he has a guru. I'm distrusting of any guru. I feel I need a teacher, a supporter, but I'm not trusting of anyone, and this may be blocking me. I don't know—how can I possibly know?

July 8

I watched Tom Hanks' *Castaway* last night, and it really felt like I could so relate to all of it. Enduring the Andaman Island jungles in India and not being able to do anything to help myself. As Tom's character says, "I had power over nothing."

I feel very scared, like I don't know which way to turn. God, please guide my every thought, word, and action.

God I need a hero's journey, a model myth of sorts. Where can I find my golden guardian angel who brings me through the pitfalls of Time? THE PITFALLS OF TIME!

Another thing that Tom Hanks' character says in the movie: "I just had to keep breathing."

And that's all I can do. Just keep breathing.

(And Nature will take care of the rest.)

Full power surrender.

July 11

I'm still communicating with Tim. We are supposed to meet in person in a few days.

Here is a list of things that I am powerless over, things that are not going right, or the way I want them to go:

- My teeth troubles
- Gaining the weight back that I lost in India
- Depression and anxiety
- Out of control, unmanageable, overwhelming feelings, including about my career
- Singing/playing guitar at my friends' wedding. I don't think I can do it. The pressure feels enormous.
- Not knowing where I want to live in the fall.
- Not having any fun. It's like I've forgotten how to have fun!
- My health, my body, my smoking, my loneliness, my depression, my

perfectionism, and whether or not I have a proper therapist, music teacher, guru, love partner.

I am powerless over whether my car breaks down or my loose tooth falls out.

Life feels unmanageable when I have a schedule, and when I don't have a schedule.

When I'm in India, and when I'm in San Francisco.

When I am thin, and when I'm average weight.

When I'm with my family, and when I'm away from my family.

When I'm in a stable apartment or living situation, and when I'm traveling or housesitting.

When I'm alone, and when I'm in a relationship.

When I'm in the fog, when I'm in the sun.

My life is completely unmanageable, and I am totally powerless over it.

I suppose I need to let go of the expectations I have of myself. All of them.

I need to drop the idea of wanting my life to be good, perfect, even happy!

The real question is: *what is underneath all this garbage?*

July 26

I haven't been writing because I've been spending all my time with Tim! We got together two weeks ago, and it's been all Tim, Tim, Tim, Tim, Tim, Tim, Tim.

"What if…?"
What if we just moved to Maui
And lived off the land and
Became true hippies and if
We had babies, we had babies oh! If
Not—fine—just be like the Garden

Of Eden—let ourselves go.
What if we just let ourselves
Go crazy, madly, deeply into the
Bliss/void?
What if I just let go and surrendered
Wholly and fully—keep the end in
Mind—this is the ONLY way we
Do it. I feel it's all good—possible—
And all will be well.

August 7

I see how the age difference is an issue with Tim, and there just isn't enough life experience there. I'm concerned. He's got a lot of humbling that will definitely be occurring over the next two years (I can see it astrologically), and oh boy, I do not know if I want to be a part of it.

I talked to Jan back in Prague yesterday, and it was such a contrast to Tim. Jan is a scrappy lad; he has had to fight for everything in his life and will continue to do so. And here I am—the thirty-six-year-old woman on the other side of the world, who is just doing her best to show up and tell the truth.

I guess the truth is… I want one more trip to India. India is my love.

I guess Tim needs to go through some hard knocks before he is ready to settle in with someone. I need to keep things in perspective; he is my lover and friend. We can definitely care for each other and help support each other, but he has got to walk this path solo—no doubt. He is clearly in a place of wanting spiritual bypassing.

August 10

I have a boyfriend now—Tim—someone who loves me, needs me, and wants to travel with me to India. This is indeed very exciting.

Tim has woken up spiritually, and it will take him several years to land. We can be teachers for each other. He teaches me about love and forgiveness, I think.

God, are you guiding me to renounce the world and GO? Is this about balance, or is it about extremes? Streamline. Put everything in storage. Sell the car.

Is Tim my soulmate or twin soul?

August 11

I need to decide whether I want to *move* to India with Tim, or return. I say move.

I'm not sure I want to tell others.

Moving to India. How to streamline stuff then?

We'll have to work from abroad to earn enough to live. Go for at least one and a half years, something like that.

Yes, I'm seriously considering *moving* to India.

August 13

Sitting around in bed the other day, taking a break from my freelance writing, I sat back and pondered, "Do I really need, WOULD I really need, all this STUFF in my life?"

I was contemplating whether to move back into San Francisco life permanently (whatever that means!) or to go off for another six months or so, back to India.

"I can't get it out of my head," so goes the old ELO song from the Seventies.

Ah, love affairs with countries...

August 17

Standing at the Crossroads...

The hardest thing for a public writer to do, oftentimes, is write while she's in the thick of something, when things are still undigested, unprocessed. Raw.

There's a fear within me that the writing is not going to make sense, that there won't be a pretty point, that it won't be enjoyed…

So where am I these days and what am I up to? I suppose I've been gathering up strength for the journey. Remember, I leaped home quite unexpectedly this last spring, pulled back to California by a force greater than me—kicked out of Ma India's nest faster than you can say "super-califragilisticexpialidocious."

It took me at least three months to land. Recovering from severe parasites, heartbreak after breaking up with Jan, and some of the most intense culture shock ever. I finally woke up, stunned, around mid-July.

Now, I'm healthy again, strong and ready to go. And I want to return to the Motherland this October, to see where She'll lead me this time…

Here's what my rational mind is telling me now:

You need to grow up.

You need to put down roots.

You need a real job.

What about a retirement plan?

Meanwhile, across town, another voice is eking to come out into the light. This is the voice of the heart.

Third time in India's a charm.

August 18

Maybe Tim is giving me a chance to do what I have always wanted to do: travel with a true partner.

August 19

I've been preparing myself for this third round of Ma India—the Divine Mother in the form of a nation, a land… a soul that resonates with mine so deeply it's impossible to ignore. I had tried to convince myself that I could, should, would hold off on my return journey to my Motherland, but that is a joke. What could possibly tear a feeding infant from the mother's breast for long? She has heard my pleas and is beckoning me back to the fold.

I came home to rebuild my strength—about ten kilos lighter and dropping boatloads of karmic weight. I've recovered from parasites and strengthened my heart, body, and soul (the mind is off wandering some-where already—don't think that element needed much strengthening!). I've also been able to digest a large dose of all that occurred for me—but it's clear that it is a case of homeopathy: I must get a bit more of the snake's venom inside of me. It's the only cure.

Thus, I'm ready to dive off the cliff. I may have a travel companion on my side, at my side this time from the get-go; it would certainly be a different approach.

August 25

I don't think I'll be fulfilled unless I go back to India.

September 3

Dear God, I'm in a really bad way, and I don't know what to do. I don't know if what I'm doing is right or wrong with or without Tim, and I am very afraid. I am scared, and I am sad, and I am powerless. God, please take my pain and suffering. I trust your will; please take it through your grace. I can't do it. Please help! I want to drop, drop, drop it all! All the persona. I need to stop, stop, STOP. Drop the role. Drop it. Because I want to die.

September 10

I feel positively lost at sea. I got on my knees to pray just now. I'm afraid I'm making a mistake. I feel like Tim is a mooring I need to have in order to be in the world. I'm so confused. I feel, at times, passively suicidal if that is possible. I feel so much self-hatred it's unreal. Why do I feel so incredibly resentful toward everything in my life? I want to get out of my life. I want to get out of SF, and that is the #1 reality.

God, I will surrender to You. I feel so completely powerless over my life that you can have it ALL.

I'm lost. Confused. Sad. Hopeless.

Do you want me to hit a bottom?

Where am I going wrong? Depressed?

I am losing my will to live. I am ready to symbolically die.

Dear God, please remove self-doubt and self-hate by your grace and mercy.

September 15

Tim and I have been together two months.

I dreamed last night he was telling me in a lofty manner how his whole heart chakra was opening. He said to me that some feel this is preparing me for a more direct transmission to the heart. Next thing I knew, I was hanging over a huge open expanse into Nothingness below me—dangling, scared—and I was about to fall into outer space forever.

September 16

We are leaving in a week for India.

When I think about meeting Tim on Craigslist, I am pretty taken aback at my apparent ability to wiggle my nose and perfectly manifest exactly what I'd always wanted:

A magnificent young man
who would up and leave
everything
and travel the world
with me!
Imagine that! He showed up!

I knew I'd be taking three trips to India (at least). I knew I wanted a loving travel partner. I just didn't know I'd be lucky enough to get both in one!

What if we were perfectly compatible, destined to meet each other in exactly the way God wants us to grow...?

September 22

One day from today, Tim and I will be boarding the big old jet airliner in the sky.

When I try to hide the anxiety I feel, it doesn't benefit anyone. Can you imagine how difficult it is to write the total and complete truth?

Well, that is what I intend to write on the journey, for it is finally dawning on me:

My life purpose is to write.

Whatever I need will be provided for.

No matter if it's on the road.

India is calling me.

In India, the truth is now calling me.

For if She weren't calling me up on the cosmic mama telephone, then you wouldn't be drawn to read this here Bohemian Ballad. As Allen Ginsberg wrote, "Bhagavan Das has never had anything better to do than to call up Mystic Mama on the Mantric Telephone."

My heart is in my throat, as I'm about to dive right into what is the biggest plunge yet taken—that of partnership while vagabond backpacking.

September 23
The Autumnal Equinox, Sun enters Libra

FEAR
Every time I leave for India
My heart leaps into my throat.
I ask myself, what the heck am I doing?
Preparing to fall down, down, down
the spiritual rabbit hole.
Did I eat the blue pill? Red pill?
Drink the elixir of Shakti, the potion that will make me feel small?
I must have faith, faith in Mother India.
Even now, when I need to be putting the final tweaks into packing,
I need to hear myself say…
It's all gonna be okay.

Packing List (In Progress)

Watch
Shoulder Bag
Passport Pouch
Dental Floss
Some Business Cards
Passport
Photocopies of Documents
Small Amount of Paper
iPod
Charger
Mini-speakers
Journal
Pen
Swiss Army Knife
Toothbrush
Toothpaste
Water Bottle
Insect Repellent
Lipstick
Tampons
Condoms
Jewelry (Few Items)
No Computer!
Tweezers
Headlamp
Batteries (Check Recharger)
Headphones
Incense Burner
One Pair of Socks
Hiking Shoes
Sleeping Bag
Pack Cover
Camera and Attachments
Sage Smudge Stick
Lighter/Matches
Sandals

Bra
Underwear
Sports Top
Bathing Suit(s)
Skirt
T-shirt
Brown Flip Flops
Meditation "Shakti" Shawl
Towel
Long Silk Tunic Top
One Pair Lycra Yoga Pants That
Will Double As Leggings
Fleece
Nail Clippers/Nail File
Zit Cream
Small Shampoo
Deodorant
Scissors
Sewing Kit
Eye Mask
Earplugs
Rescue Remedy Sleep
Night Guard
Rescue Remedy Regular
Band-Aids
Emergency Dental Crown Stuff
Doctor/Health Info List
Contact List
Allergy List
Travel Insurance
Insurance Info
Supplements Including:
Grapefruit Seed Extract
Traveler's Friend Water Drops
Echinacea/Golden Seal Probiotics

Love Is Ablaze

San Francisco
September 23, 2007

Have you ever fallen in love?
In love with a place?
A place in time and space.
You can never forget Her face.
She pulls, beckons, tears at your heart.
You'll give everything, go to any lengths
For just one more chance to see Her.
Your true Beloved.
Her name is India.

For some of us, that Beloved is Ma India.

Yesterday, drinking my coffee in the September sunshine of San Francisco, I received an email from a fellow Indophile and blog fan. All it said—all it had to say—was:

"So, Erin, when are you headed back to The Motherland?"

My heart crunched, ached, contracted, swooned!

How could you resist such a pull?

Your very Mother, who teaches you so.

Scolds you, molds you, sears your very soul.

I am so ready to return to Her. I already feel my sandals pitter-pat on the paths of the dusty markets, worn soles upon the soul of the earth.

I can smell the huge pots of oil frying, the incense, the cow dung—
the essence of *eau d'India*, an intoxicating concoction of aromas like no
other seeps into my pores.

The sacred Mother's earth beneath my feet.

Ever grounding me, pulling my roots down deep.

The saints, sadhus, priests, and pilgrims loudly, unabashedly sing
praises:

Ram Ram Sita Ram

Sita Ram Sita Ram

Jaya Hanuman!

After six long months of waiting, I've recovered from parasites, cobra
encounters, and sand flea attacks.

Six months later, I've regained my physical and mental steadiness, and
I'm ready to plunge in again.

Six months later, I am ready to undertake the THIRD epic journey to
the Motherland. Time for takeoff!

A spark has been caught in the wind.

Love, sweet love is ablaze

And you're off again!

Service with a Smile
Delhi
September 26, 2007

Three a.m., India Standard Time. Middle of the night. Tim and I have just touched down in Delhi's Indira Gandhi International Airport, beat and bedraggled from our thirty-six-hour intercontinental haul.

While Tim waits for our rucksacks to tumble into the baggage carousel, I skip off to the first loo in sight. A bespectacled, twenty-something Chinese girl tails me into the toilets.

"Hello?" she gets my attention. Bleary-eyed and exhausted, I turn around to face her half asleep and inquisitive.

"Where going?" she inquires somewhat timidly, but smilingly, in broken English. I get the feeling she's mustering up some courage.

"Right now?" I respond. "To the bathroom." I'm eager to make it to the restroom as I've already been delayed beyond my bladder limit.

"No, after."

"You mean, tonight?"

"No, after," she clarifies. I figure out she wants my India itinerary while I'm merely focused on navigating the smelly squat toilets.

"Oh. Well, likely we are headed to Dharamshala after a couple of nights in Delhi. But we really have no idea."

"Me too!" she responds happily. "I come with you?"

Now, I do want to help her. Of course, my heart goes out to solo women travelers, being a veteran myself. Yet, I'm not sure I want to be assigned instant chaperone status before I even clear customs.

Still, it's 3 a.m., it's obviously this young woman's first excursion on the subcontinent, and I'll certainly do my best to get her off to a strong start.

"I can help you get to a hotel tonight. After, I have no idea what our plans are."

"Okay!" She lights up with glee.

I hurry out to baggage claim, where Tim and I cheer as our bags have successfully followed us through a tricky Taipei transfer. As we cross through Immigration toward the exit, the young Chinese woman scurries to join us at the pre-paid taxi stand.

"Hi!" she greets us. "I have no money! What do I do?"

I am too tired to start this trip off as a bona fide babysitter.

"You need to go to the currency exchange and get yourself some rupees. So you can get a taxi." I point out the Thomas Cooke counter over yonder.

"Oh! Okay!" And she's off into the shuffle for her first lesson in late-night arrivals. Tim and I wait for her to return. Our exhaustion levels are peaking, and when she fails to come back after a long wait, we finally decide she'll have to go with God, and we'll keep an eye for her at the curb while we wait for our taxi.

A few minutes later, standing in the taxi queue, another young woman pops over to us, asking if we'll let her hop in our cab. She explains that she hasn't gotten a taxi voucher yet, and no, she hasn't a destination hotel. I notice her slight Canadian accent. She's quite well-mannered and patient, given it is 3 a.m. and must also be exhausted. Meanwhile, the hassling cabbie cons are trying to divert our attention from our official taxi, getting in our faces like nagging gnats or flies one must swat at.

As I'm trying to speak to the Canadian woman to explain how to get to a decent hotel in the backpacker district, one particularly irritating tout is bopping in and out of our conversation—and our minimal personal space—with increasing volume and rudeness.

"Shut up!" the Canadian woman suddenly screams at the jerk, calling him off like the feral dog he is. Then, without missing a beat, she turns a bright smile back on me to convince us that we should let her join us for the night.

At this point, I'm done. Besides, this gal is obviously a seasoned traveler. If she can tell a con man off like that without missing a beat, she can definitely hold her own.

Like I said, my heart goes out to solo travelers; I have been there many times. But there's a shower, and a bed, and a reservation, gods-be-willing, with our names on them, and I'm just no longer up for playing Mother India in the middle of the night.

I let out a long sigh—I didn't realize I was so tired—and tell the Canadian gal, "I'm really sorry. We really need to go now and be on our way. I know you understand. I know you'll get where you're going just fine. The hotels I told you about in Pahar Ganj are reliable. You'll be fine."

"Sure. I get it," she said, sincerely. And she did.

Boundaries are so useful.

Besides, I had already played Good Samaritan before even getting off the plane, having been requested by a China Airlines flight attendant to file a statement with the Indian airport police as witness to a crime.

It was a serious crime by airline standards. As our plane descended from 30,000 to 10,000 to zero feet, a mysterious ringing began to sound incessantly above my head.

The stewardesses were visibly alarmed (which never makes passengers feel at ease), shaking up the sleepy travelers that sat under the luggage compartment.

Was a bomb about to blow? The flight attendants scrambled to locate the culprit bag—the source of the sound of danger—as our plane descended quickly. They needed to get back and strapped into their own jump seats.

"Whose bag is this?" the China Airlines senior purser barked as she held up a nondescript black shoulder bag. The black bag was ringing.

Someone had left a cell phone on in the overhead compartment directly over my head.

"Hello! Whose bag is this?"

A few seats ahead of us, a drowsy Indian admitted that, yes, he was the culprit. The chief flight attendant gave him a loud lecture in a pissed-off Chinese accent—one hell of a talking-to that the entire pack of passengers was to witness.

"Sir! You have committed a serious air traffic offense. You will be the last one to leave the plane. You will be questioned by the Delhi Airport Police. We do not know what measures will be taken. Your fate will be left to the authorities."

His pleas of innocence—that it was an honest mistake, an oversight—held no weight. This Chief Madam of China Airlines would have none of it.

Since the bag was found above my seat, I was chosen as the best witness of said crime and was asked to give a statement. Upon disembarking, Tim and I were held captive, cornered at the fuselage exit and made to wait for the Indian police—a grand reminder, before even hitting Indian soil, that packing a full bag of humor is an absolute necessity for travel.

The China Airlines staff expressed profuse apologies as we awaited the authorities at the ramp: "So sorry, madam. Thank you for your cooperation."

I smiled sleepily back. "No problem. I'm sure we'll be upgraded to first class the next time we fly with China Airlines, yes?"

But of course!

Now that's SERVICE WITH A SMILE.

Om Away from Om
Delhi
September 27, 2007

The morning after arriving in India, I perched on the rooftop terrace of our guest house with nowhere to go, nothing to do. Blue skies with clouds parting. Weather a perfect 85 degrees F with a pleasant breeze in Delhi. Same old smell of curries mixed with wafts of incense and dung. Generators running and gurgling as the power alternated, surging on and off. I made a note in my journal.

Sitting beside Tim in the cab ride to the Hare Krishna Guest House—my Delhi "om away from om"—I reflect on what occurred in the airport and marvel at the magnet I must be to travelers. This time, I'm not even dressed as an experienced gypsy yet. I'm wearing REI high-tech fabric capris and a North Face fleece—but somehow, people want to ask me the whys and hows of getting around. It's starting to hit me that I've just come here with a one-way ticket and zero plans.

Maybe I need work. Maybe I need a task. Like, what the hell am I doing back here so soon? What can I do? How may I serve? Do I need to serve those here, or those back home?

I feel a bit of fear. I feel a concern I'm going to be bored and unsettled. Hence the need for a project. Actually a life project. I realize how anxious and unsettled I am.

The answer came:

My only "work" here is to learn to stay in the present.

While Tim slept, I went off by myself to my favorite restaurant in Pahar Ganj, where I was greeted immediately with, "Good to see you again!" I could hardly believe these people remember me. It was so refreshing. The little waiter boy. Such a sweet face and huge smile. I was deeply touched. Suddenly, I realized I am so very lucky, and I swooned inside, my soul breathing a sigh of relief.

"I'm Glad We Ain't Amish"
Delhi
September 28, 2007

Last night we were kept awake by the Vietnamese young man in the room above us, who traveled with his karaoke machine. All night, strains of M.C. Hammer's "Can't Touch This," Blondie's "The Tide is High," and R. Kelly's "I Believe I Can Fly" reverberated throughout the guest house. When we met him in the hall to ask him how it is to travel with a huge karaoke machine, his response came quickly:

"It gets the girls in my room."

Can't argue with that.

Three days into Delhi, we've alternated between daily tasks of booking trains, sampling *lassis,* and recovering from severe jetlag. Between our minimal jaunts into the hectic (putting it mildly), grimy (putting it really mildly) streets of the Pahar Ganj Main Bazaar, we've sat and/or reclined in the nude, fairly motionless, on our bed all day, the ceiling fan constantly blowing full blast. We're also taking three showers a day, anything to stay fairly clean and relatively cool—and sane. We've only donned clothing when absolutely necessary to leave our room. Being extra careful to close the door to the main hallway lest we reveal our situation to the other guests, it was an ongoing joke.

"I'm glad we're not Mennonite," Tim says, referring to the Amish man we saw with Teva sandals and a fanny pack during our layover in the Taipei airport. Following up, he said, "I'm glad we ain't Amish."

I can't stop cracking up. Punch-drunk on jet lag, it's the funniest thing I've ever heard.

Tomorrow, we catch a train to Rishikesh, further north on the holy Ganges.

The Land of Seers
Rishikesh
October 4, 2007

Admitting to myself that I'll never be able to convey all the tales in my brain, nor the visceral experiences in my veins, I'll suffice with a meek attempt to convey a tiny droplet of the ever-flowing, all-powerful Ganges of consciousness. I have gotten clear that my only "work" while I am in India is to learn to stay in the present.

Early October, beautiful light. Tim and I are quaintly, cozily nestled in, here in Rishikesh at the base of the Himalayas, at the source of the great river goddess, Ganga. *Rishis* were the ancient seers of India, those who directly received the sacred texts pointing to Reality—the Vedas.

This is my adopted North India OM away from home. It's my fourth pilgrimage to this holy land, the self-proclaimed "yoga capital of the world." Ah, sweet Rishikesh—land of seers, sages, and saints—a particularly comfy place to begin or end one's Indian journey, whether a veteran, seasoned traveler, or newbie to the nation, as I was the first time I came here five years ago. Rishikesh remains a great place to cut one's India travel teeth on food and culture, religion and philosophy, customs and chaos. All in all, a gentle starting point on the path.

The village of Lakshman Jhula, where we now reside, is filled with temples, *sadhus* and *babas*, renunciates, pilgrims, travelers and teachers.

A variety of yoga classes start and end each day at the plethora of ash-rams, all for just $1.00 to $2.25 per class—quite the bargain compared to San Francisco's new wave yoga studio prices. Here, you can take your pick of the lot, from kundalini to tantra, Iyengar to pranayama or Siva-nanda hatha style.

But here, the point is not to compare yoga teachers or fads; to me, practicing yoga in Rishikesh means gaining the gift of grooving with a real yogi. It's not about how hip my spandex is, nor about getting wash-board abs to look hot in a midriff. Here, I'm soaking in tradition, devo-tion, and prayer along with my asana practice.

Strangely, I can turn myself upwards into a headstand or full back-bend here much easier than in a California yoga studio. Competition disappears. Doubt and fear have exited the building. There's just as much reason to be able to *do* the posture as there is reason to be physically in-capable; mind over matter, if you will. Sounds odd, I know, but somehow I feel more confident on holy ground.

Holy, indeed. To me, there's no question that God/Goddess/All-That-Is (the universal energy force) is alive, awake, and enthusiastically at the helm in Rishikesh. This is a vortex, created by a trine between the riv-er Ganga and two majestic, magical mountain points to the north and south representing yin and yang: Nanda Devi, the Bliss-Giving Goddess and Neelkanth Mahadev, the sacred masculine in the form of Shiva.

From the balcony of our room at San Sewa Ashram, overlooking the river, it is quite clear that the *prana* (also known as chi, or life force en-ergy) is in full throttle at this planetary power spot. It's easy to spend hours in surprisingly effortless meditation, simply staring into seem-ingly empty space. With just a tiny shift in awareness, it's possible to see the wavelets and rivulets of light energy squiggling, shooting, sparking across the airwaves. Frankly, it's psychedelic!

Of course, this life force is present everywhere. Yet in such a place as Rishikesh, it's concentrated and visible to the naked eye. How? Why? There is always the Great Mystery—answers that are ineffable. And yet, it's quite clear to me that it's a divine symbiosis: Mother Nature's perfection in placement of yin and yang power spots. Thousands upon thousands of years of pilgrimages, prayers, love and sheer devotion offered to God and Goddess, reflected back into the hearts, minds, eyes, and souls of the trusting. In such prime conditions, consciousness is raised and awakened to unfathomable levels.

Tim and I are quite aware that we are blessed to be here, and we are blessing this place in return. Soaking it all in, and, hopefully, contributing in our own small way—whether through simple awareness or our own individual *puja* rituals.

Daily, we seem to be attracting sadhus, swamis, and sages like moths to flame, butterflies to *amrita*—divine nectar.

The Richest Man in Rishikesh
Rishikesh
October 11, 2007

Tim and I continue to abide in the holiest land of the saints. *Hare Om!* I believe we'll be here for a good while longer. Hardly a reason to rush, and no reason to tear oneself away prematurely from the cradle of the Ganga Herself.

Amongst the variety of sadhus and sages we've been gifted to have met, perhaps the most radiant, brilliant light has been the beatific baba on the banks of the Ganga. He is called Baba Ram Das—not to be confused with Richard Alpert, aka Ram Dass, that is…

A few days after our arrival in Lakshman Jhula, Tim and I were sitting at the riverside, meditating and soaking in the radiant vibrations. I happened to notice a brilliant white light out of the corner of my right eye, about ten meters away.

The light emanated off a holy man, a boisterous baba with a long white beard and white *lungi* (sarong-like garment). The translucent baba was attempting to communicate his heart's passion to a cluster of bikini-clad Israeli girls who were plopped on a beach blanket, munching crisps and smoking smokes.

"All… God! God… All!" I heard the baba pronounce heartily, with a merry twinkle in his eye. The Israeli girls grinned back through oversized Dior knockoff sunglasses.

Nice, I thought. Simple message. Seems to be a bright spark coming from him. Doesn't look to be bumming smokes or chai money. Just sharing the love.

I turned back to watch Tim, who was knee-deep in holy water a few feet out into the river, praying to the river goddess. Suddenly, the same baba appeared at my left shoulder, seated in full lotus position, chest risen slightly, hands in meditation mudra, smiling at me with sheer glee. I was slightly startled, but after I saw he only wanted to share meditation, I relaxed into my own sitting posture.

Tim strode out of the water to join us, and Baba began our personal teaching session spontaneously, unsolicited. His English consisted of a random selection of words and hand gestures that were rudimentary, charming... and we got exactly what he meant. But the most important thing he transmitted to us was LIGHT. And I'm talking BRIGHT.

Every time he motioned toward us, it was like a fantasy movie image. His finger would come toward me, but it was followed by sparks and trails, like an LSD flashback from a 1960's film. He was a character from a spiritual science fiction movie.

After sussing out the situation, we determined that Baba was definitely on to something good, so when he invited us to his hut just up the hill, we happily obliged and felt honored to enter his home.

Baba had an agenda. He wanted to teach us the essence of unified Shiva (consciousness) and Shakti (form), the divine intertwine of yang and yin. He had a very clear image to convey:

"Man..." he would say, pointing at Tim, "rain!"

"Woman..."—directing an impossibly long finger at me—"earth!"

Then, he'd start giggling and cracking himself up. We'd start giggling and cracking up, too. So, he'd continue.

"Man... One time. Give Earth. Rain. Make Flowers!"

Every time he meant to say the English word "after," he would say "before," which was right in line with the perfectly paradoxical methods of instruction, leaving much to the creative imagination.

Then, his teachings got even more sophisticated. Baba was very clear on the right time for sex, the method, and the route to bliss—it's surprising how much can come through with sign language!

"You..." he said, pointing to my *yoni* area (pelvic region) with his foot-long index finger. "Before 'lady juice' time (remember: "before" means "after")... One, two, three day. Your culture, seven day!"

I got it; I knew "lady juice" meant menses. Baba continued:

"After lady juice, bathing. Washing. Man. Woman. Together. Man, top. Woman, under."

Like I said, very specific.

"Man, no finish! Woman... one, two, three times finish! You, strong!" Nodding to Tim. "No sleeping!" Then, to me, "You get stronger!"

We both knew what he was referring to, having read a small amount on tantric sexual practices.

Baba delighted that Tim and I were indeed grasping all he was passing on with energetic effort. "I read..." he continued, pointing to a huge stack of Hindi and Sanskrit books—yogic and philosophical texts—lying on his musty shelves just inside the door of his humble little home. "I read... your culture!"

So Baba knew the problems and challenges of Western love, marriage, and sex. It appeared he was doing his darndest to help whatever individuals and pairs might cross his blessed path.

The love emanating from this holy man was so strong, Tim and I would just zonk out when he gazed into our eyes with his bliss. We were in love. We *were* love!

Ram Das appeared to be a bigger baba than we thought. We stood in the small clearing outside his little home, and while Baba showed us a couple handstands that would make your head spin, a group of middle-class Indian men was starting down the jungle path toward the hut.

From the minuscule Hindi I could catch (a bit of Sanskrit gleaned over the years from yoga and meditation studies helps), I comprehended that these locals were coming to pay respects to Baba Ram Das. They were hoping to receive *darshan*, or blessings. So this was no random homeless holy man, and certainly no amateur sadhu shacked up by the river.

Baba's eyes twinkled as he gaily explained to them in melodious, lilting Hindi that he was obviously giving teachings to two V.I.P. guests (motioning toward the two of us) in a private audience. The locals would have to come back tomorrow since we, the adopted students of the afternoon, were receiving priority. It dawned on me that our time with this saint was a spontaneous gift.

Baba made quite clear to us several times that he wanted absolutely no money for his teachings. Only humble offerings of chai, chapati flour, dal, and rice from the market would be accepted—and only one time. "Baba no money, no taking. You, only giving."

A-ha. He wasn't taking. We were giving. I liked that.

At one point, Baba looked directly into my eyes and said valiantly, "You... Teacher!"

"Um... yes, Babaji," I replied, using *ji* to denote respect. "Sort of. I am writer."

"You... BIG MIND," he continued. "You... teacher. You... looking. Seeing... Guru, guru, guru. Knowing. Good guru. Bad guru. You KNOW!"

I got it, or at least I think I got it. Baba was implying that with my wisdom, or "big mind," I could sense instantly whether a "teacher" met on the river or on the road, in temples or towns, was a false prophet or the real deal. "Yes, Babaji, I know!" I responded.

"YES!" He leaned back and giggled with sheer glee, completely pleased that he had successfully analyzed me, and having a grand time entertaining himself. "YES! Big Mind!" And with that, he stretched out his rail-thin, muscled yogi arms, wiggled his impossibly long fingers, and began to enthusiastically massage my temples with such vigor that I knew he was shaking loose a few more marbles, or at least dusting out a few cobwebs of cloudy thought.

Now, I would normally never let a stranger toy with my temples, third eye, or any such sensitive point without asking permission first (there's a reason they're called "temples," being gateways to God). Yet, true to Baba's reading of me, I do know when I'm in good hands, and whom to trust, and when. And I was all too happy to let this beautiful, enlightened being illuminate my consciousness, free my mind, and shake up the shakti.

Baba's eyes exuded the luminescence of a thousand suns. He had It. Drunk on life, 24/7. Blissed out. Celibate and married in divine union with God. Riches beyond compare. Who needs paper money or plastic rupees when you've got the infinite riches of the universe within?

This is the Baba on the Bank of the Ganges. A bank with unlimited wealth. An inexhaustible storehouse to be drawn from anytime, constantly regenerating and invigorating itself.

That night, both Tim and I experienced lucid dreams, or astral "encounters," if you will, with the Baba on the Banks.

In the dreamtime, I walked down to the riverside and chatted further with His Preciousness. In the morning, Tim awakened to describe his face-to-face encounter with Baba in the astral realms: "Baba's light was so bright. His being simply blew me away. He IS light."

Most yogis who reach an exalted state of enlightenment prefer to hide away high in the Himalayas, to be disturbed by no one, least of all random travelers and rowdy backpackers. Yet, every so often, one of these holy men decides, or rather it is decided by the Great Unseen, that such radiance remain close to civilization, to act as a wayshower, a ray of hope, a beacon and guide to illuminate the way.

For this, I offer gratitude and appreciation to Baba Ram Das and All-That-Is, for blessing Tim and me with an incomparable embodiment of Divine Beauty, Pure Love, and Sheer Light.

Animal Planet
Rishikesh
October 20, 2007

You never know when something as uneventful as getting a leg wax is going to bring new friends into the fold. For the past two weeks, we've been hobnobbing with the local beautician—a young widow named Reena—and her family, learning Indian cooking (household staples such as aloo gobi—cauliflower and potato masala – and lentil dal) with a bonus side course of unsolicited, juicy village gossip.

We are now renting an apartment (which happens to be nestled safely behind the police station) in the complex of a well-respected family, that of the retired postmaster. We've got three rooms—full bath with hot water, full kitchen, and bedroom—for 150 rupees ($2) a night. And there are two healthy cows serving up fresh milk twice a day.

We are the only Westerners in our little compound. Except for the sounds of the neighboring Indian family living less than three feet from our window (we hear every cough and cricket game) and our next-door yoga teacher smashing ginger on the counter to make chai at the crack of dawn, the only sounds are the tinkling temple bells, chirping crickets, and morning moos as the cows are milked.

We've got a little Animal Planet in our flat, too. Two of the largest arachnid relatives I've ever seen have shacked up in our bathroom. We've nicknamed them Boris (after The Who's song, "Boris the Spider") and Natasha.

The spiders living in the loo have a circumference the size of a large hand. They are hairier than a hound with eight legs. They like to get our heart pounding by startling us on the doorknob, by the showerhead, or directly on the squat toilet.

For the first few days, Tim was literally scared shitless to go to the bathroom. In all honesty, I suppose I would have been, too, but life in the Andaman Islands jungles sort of cured me last year. Once cobras creep into your camp, sharing digs with a gargantuan Charlotte does not seem like the worst roommate placement after all.

Swami Scoldings
Rishikesh
October 21, 2007

We did not expect that our visit to the local meditation cave would be the source of our deep, rich purification. No matter who—or what—the inhabitants of our bathroom, soon enough, we'd have to get real cozy, real quick with the loo...

This was to be my second visit to the Vasistha Gufa cave, my first being in 2002. I wanted to take Tim there, as I remembered the spiritual vibrations in the meditation cave to be very strong.

An educative swami in the village reminded me how to get there, via local bus on a hair-pinned, winding road about twelve miles upriver. Swamiji told us the importance of the cave—how the great guru Vasistha was the guru of the god Rama in his early years. The sage Vasistha himself meditated in this cave during the time of Rama, between 900 to 800 BC.

As mentioned, we are currently shacked up in the apartment next door to a yoga teacher, Krishna Swami, who teaches a lovely hatha class on our rooftop each morn. We informed Swami that we'd be missing class the following day for our cave field trip.

He didn't seem thrilled about our excursion. At all.

Stopping Tim on his way out of class, Swami questioned, "Which swami told you to go to the cave?"

Apparently dissatisfied with Tim's reply, Swami continued. "You know, you have no need to go to the cave. You want to be in the cave? Meditate. Here. You may also be in the cave, but your mind will be here. Makes no difference. No need to go to the cave."

Rubbish, Tim and I declared to each other once we were behind closed doors. We figured he's just persnickety because we'd been talking to other teachers.

And off we went! We were most excited about our excursion, fortuitously timed, sitting in meditation in the cave at the exact time of the New Moon.

Three days later, Tim and I were both sick in bed from chills and diarrhea, and yoga headstands were the last things on our minds. One morning, as Tim made a brief appearance outdoors to hang laundry, Swami Krishna again confronted him in the garden gateway.

"When I am speaking to you, it is Krishna talking to you! You shouldn't have gone to the cave. I told you. Now you're purifying."

Certainly, I didn't know what to make of this implied ownership of our *chela* (student) discipleship. Knowingly or unknowingly, we had moved into Krishna Swami's mini-ashram, and therefore, we were subject to and expected to abide by the teachings and guidance of Krishna Swami. And the result of our ignorance? Toilet troubles.

Needless to say, once Delhi Belly sets in, fears must be faced. No matter how big, how hairy, or how scary the spiders in the loo, when you gotta go, you gotta go. Tim and I made fast friends with Boris and Natasha.

Luckily, even Krishna—*especially* Lord Krishna—has compassion. In fact, Krishna's the best at the *bhakti* (devotional love).

Our mutual illness gave Tim and me ample opportunity to play nurse and doctor, caring for each other, learning to love in a new way, with good humor and bad bathroom jokes.

Spiritual purification, instant karma, or just plain India. Whatever you call it, it's practically a given that sooner or later you're going to get hit with a bug.

A sense of humor gets a traveler through—make the best of bed rest, or it will get the best of you!

Fear of Non-Doing
Rishikesh
October 22, 2007

In spite of attempting to get along well with Tim, I feel stressed and confused. These are all great moments, enjoying beautiful people and experiences in India; but I am conflicted. I wonder if it would be so much easier being alone, if I could figure it all out better on my own. Privately, in the safety of my journal, I try to console myself:

FEAR OF NON-DOING

How am I doing, really? Do I understand my "purpose" for being in India this time around?

What shall I accomplish besides, ironically, the art of non-doing?

I know it takes a long time to decompress from the West. At first, one dreams of people back home, as the mind progresses, detoxes, and categorizes the past, juxtaposed against the new vibration of thought patterns of the East—or non-thought as it were.

Why do I come here?

To be. To allow myself to breathe, away from capitalism and the pressures of money—earning and productivity. Even so, I can't entirely leave my Western nature behind, as I ask myself each day what small thing I might accomplish, even if it is simply reading, writing a new story, or doing my washing in a guest house bucket.

Why do I come here?

To be close to the earth, to Nature, at all times. India, which is about seventy percent rural, lives close to the ground. Most Indians live outdoors a large chunk of the day, doing their laundry, cooking, minding the dairy cows, or tending to their chai stand, for example.

Why do I come here?

To learn new things about the world and life as a whole. To love, and to be love. To be loved, and to be loving.

The Ghost of George Harrison
Rishikesh
October 20, 2007

For the third time (in this life), I visited the dilapidated Maharishi Mahesh Yogi Ashram in Rishikesh. The Maharishi imbued his teachings of Transcendental Meditation (TM) to the Beatles in the late 1960s. The resultant musical influence and subsequent gift to the world? *The White Album.*

As for me, I love visiting the abandoned ashram grounds; the place resonates with history and mystery. So when Tim expressed an interest in seeing the Ashram, I willingly obliged to play tour guide. Only, I was not willing to pay *baksheesh* to the scary ghoul at the gate extorting cash upon entrance to the grounds. I wanted to risk NO chance of the man recognizing me from our face-off the year prior, when we got into a heavy tiff. I captured this righteous 'n' rowdy encounter in *The Adventures of Bindi Girl*, in a chapter entitled "Maa Durga and the Tiger."

Thus, to avoid an altercation, Tim and I sought another entrance route. We scaled the jungle walls on the backside of the ashram property, with the waves of the Ganges lapping along the bluffs. We caught the attention of a lingering sadhu, living along the shores of the river goddess, to see if he could help us figure out how to get in.

"Ashram upside?" We motioned to an overgrown path leading up the hill.

"*Haan*," was the sadhu's affirmative reply.

Covered with burrs and brambles, creatures, and other questionable things was a sketchy route up the cliff into the ashram grounds. It seemed more suitable for sows, goats and cows than spiritual questers, no matter how determined they were to scale the joint.

The sweet holy man spoke a few words of English and was kind enough to most sincerely explain that we should know in advance that "there are no more Beatles inside."

Tim and I were not deterred. Crawling under spiderwebs seeming fit for the Amazon rainforest, we flipped and flopped in wet, muddy sandals up the side of the mountain. As we neared the top, we found ourselves overlooking a crop of meditation pod-huts. Overgrown with jungle foliage, the pods resembled living abodes from *Lord of the Rings*— or *Lord of the Flies*.

Tim chided me as we crawled up the cliff. "This is nuts, Erin. Are you sure we can do this? You ARE crazy."

"It's cool," I half-whispered back. I actually *was* nervous about getting spotted by the gatekeeper, thinking perhaps I should have just paid the man his bribe and had a peaceful, easy entrance.

"We gotta get out before sunset. It's getting dark fast. There's no way I'm going back down that slope in the dark with all those spiders," declared Tim, the more sensible adventurer.

"We'll hurry," I promised. I wanted to show Tim the underground meditation cells in the ruins of the grand meditation hall, where the Maharishi would hold TM court.

As we hustled toward the larger buildings jutted against the jungle, I feared we'd run into a villager warning us about tigers, which would really put Tim over the edge. We struggled to get through the dangling lianas above our heads, the neck-high needle bushes, and the wild wisps of spiderwebs.

Everything looked so different than the last time I was here. I couldn't recognize the building shapes, and daylight was disappearing rapidly. My heart was beating fast and I felt a bit panicked; I couldn't find the main hall. "We'd better turn back," I admitted defeat. I hated to let him down.

"It's okay," Tim responded. "Let's just get the hell out of here before it gets any darker."

Turning on our heels, heading out the opposite direction, we came upon a sudden sight that nearly made us, well, *lose it*.

Before our eyes was a middle-aged Indian peasant who had just come out of the jungle after a long day's work with the machete. He'd popped a *bidi* (hand-rolled tobacco leaf) smoke in his mouth, pulled up his lungi, and settled himself comfortably amongst the vines, crouching low in a squat to enjoy a nice, luxurious shit—known in India as a "long toilet."

At the sight of two random white folks moving towards him from out of nowhere, he looked as if he'd seen a spook. Pulling down his lungi in a state of near-shock and panic at our presence, the peasant ran off into the jungle without a backward glance.

"We scared the shit out of him!" Tim and I giggled devilishly, like two mischievous schoolchildren that were pushing their limits—and we were. We did not have a flashlight, and the night creatures had already started their vocal performance, complete with monkey-cacophony. Darkness was falling swiftly. Plus, I was terrified that the Blue Meanie of a gatekeeper would discover us and (worse) remember me, and I did not want a repeat performance of the previous year's monkey- and wall-scaling in order to escape. "Let's go, Tim!" I urged.

We were walking briskly toward the exit path when the hair rose on the back of my neck. Wafting through the foliage began the most delicate stringed melody: the unmistakable thirteen-note intro to "Norwegian Wood."

Instantly, the lyrics appeared in my mind's ear:
I once had a girl
Or should I say
She once had me.
The unmistakable twang of guitar made to croon like George Harrison's

sitar! Coming from nowhere! We had thought that we were the only ones around the ashram; we hadn't seen a soul except for the squatting jungle man.

Whether it was George-come-from-the-grave, or a brave, camped-out hippie in a hut, something was definitely doing some strumming in the vicinity.

She showed me her room
Isn't it good?
Norwegian wood.

We were transfixed. "Is that a ghost?" I half joked.

"I don't know," Tim replied, "but where is that guitar coming from?"

We couldn't see anyone in the fading light, and we were still concerned about getting out in time. "We better go!" I said.

Then, as if to confirm that all was right with the world, that we were in the exact right place at the exact right time, next came the strums of "Here Comes the Sun," Harrison's *Abbey Road* jewel.

I was beginning to think that someone had spiked my morning chai with Lucy in the Sky.

Mesmerized, Tim and I enjoyed a sublime cocktail of a magical music moment, with fear chaser. Even though our mystery guitar man was perched and plucking somewhere very nearby, singing up the sun, in our immediate world it was nearing dusk rapidly. We wanted to remain at our phantom concert, undisturbed save for the calls of cicadas, or perhaps seek out the source of the specter's sounds.

Yet the threat of entrapment inside the gates loomed strong. We had to choose. Deciding to leave the musical spirit to rest in peace, we bid a silent adieu to the Ghost of George Harrison and swiftly moved out of the grounds, scaling the cliff path back to safety, the sun setting like a giant orange orb over the Ganges.

It was a perfect final evening in Rishikesh.

Advaita Angst
Lucknow
October 24, 2007

Crossing west to east across north India, en route to Varanasi, we stopped in Lucknow, the unassuming capital of Uttar Pradesh state. We were staying a few days at the family home and mahasamadhi (burial place of a realized sage) of one of Tim's gurus—H.W.L. Poonja, known as Papaji.

Outwardly attempting to get along with my young lover, the tension with Tim was growing as I felt increasingly frustrated, agitated, and irritable with self and other. On top of that, being involved with someone who had a guru confused me even more. I arose extra early to write in my journal and try to make myself feel better:

Surya the Sun is rising fast on the horizon this morning, and I'm up early and writing. I am really getting into reading about Advaita (non-dual wisdom) here at Papaji's house in Lucknow. Advaita is perhaps best expressed as Piscean dissolving, all returning back to the Source. Advaita means "not two"—oneness. Some say it's really advanced spiritual and should only be attempted once the person has accumulated plenty of merit.

I don't know if I've accumulated merit and what that would mean anyway!

I feel so much resentment and anger bubbling deep inside my cells. It is contentless and roiling in the body, liquid hot. I wonder if this is what is meant by *tapas* (burning of impurities)? What is this seething anger and incredible frustration being projected at Tim? It comes up especially around the Guru Question—to have a guru or have not a guru.

Astrologically, I am experiencing transiting Pluto conjunct my natal Venus in Sagittarius, in the Seventh House of relationships and partnerships—that could be the anger. If it is Pluto/Hades inflaming me, well, then, there is absolutely nothing, nothing at all that can be done about it, except leave Tim and go on my merry way. I feel like Pluto on personal planets portends a hell of a lot of suffering.

Can Tim and I really get along, ever, or are we destined to a life of fighting and arguing?

Why do I feel so resistant and angry toward my partner? It is all under the surface, showing up as little barbs and jabs, a general unhappiness and depression deep in my soul.

I feel powerless over this, so I feel like the best thing I can do is to make myself feel relatively comfortable while we're together.

I have become completely saturated with all this "spiritual" or non-spiritual junk that is going on, and yet it is me. I want to stay with Tim, and yet I feel I need to go. My soul wants to fly solo because I am so miserable. Tim wants me to take a side trip and go to Ayodhya, where Ram and Hanuman and Sita originated, without him—alone—because I keep venting about how much I need time and space apart. I feel so confused. Is it really necessary to separate?

Every now and then, I feel I have to go do something wild, off the beaten path, something not on the *Lonely Planet* guidebook route. I feel eternally dissatisfied, and that includes dissatisfied with Tim and my relationship with Tim. I wonder, is that because I am just an unsatisfied person? Why am I so angry? Why am I so judgmental? Are enlightened people better people? Better to be around? I have at least two or three friends who lay claim to enlightenment and several dozen more who have had enlightenment experiences, albeit under the influence of psychedelia or peak experiences such as merging, divine union, or bliss—during sex, mountain climbing, music experiences, dream states, or (in my own case) running a marathon.

Two things are pressing on me right now:

1. Feelings about traveling with Tim vs. alone

2. Feelings about gurus/discipleship. I haven't yet met anyone where I've been like, "I want YOU to be my teacher. I respect you enough. I like what you're saying, I like the philosophy..." or a person who has floored me with emotion or spirit. In America, we are taught to think for ourselves, but do we really?

"What does your life stand for?" Tim's female Advaita teacher, Gangaji, queries. Well, my life doesn't seem to stand for much lately, yet if I go a little deeper, I see that indeed I stand for courage, adventure, faith, and trust in the human spirit.

What do I need? How can I be fulfilled? How may I serve?

Flow. Flow is important. I need to feel like a teacher to myself. If I am a teacher, I wonder what my sangha needs. Perhaps I am the guru to myself, and I need to start treating this life as my faithful sangha? Or maybe I'm simply full of crud and none of it really matters. I don't know. I feel like I'm filled with judgment.

Yes, I need a break. After Lucknow, I think I will go to Ayodhya alone and meet up with Tim in Varanasi afterward. Maybe a side trip will help me clear out this nauseating, gnashing internal conflict.

At the Guru's House
Lucknow
October 25, 2007

It is in Lucknow that I began to deepen my understanding of the first of Buddha's Four Noble Truths:

There is suffering.

We've all heard it. Suffering is a part of life.

Now, you may disagree, as I am prone to do. I like to play around and fool myself; I like to be Pollyanna in my thinking, focus on the positive. I like to think of Abraham Lincoln's saying, "Most people are as happy as they make up their minds to be."

All true, yes. But the common thread between each and every one of us souls on the planet is that there is suffering. Some of us suffer externally, through physical pain, poverty, loss, and the like. Most of us from the Western world, however, seem to suffer internally, through depression, angst, worry, lust, regret—the trials of the human psyche.

If you're human, you suffer, taught the Buddha. It's part of the deal.

Luckily, the Buddha didn't stop at the First Noble Truth. He—and a host of other enlightened beings throughout time—also taught that there is a way out. There is freedom from craving, freedom from aversion. You know—all that non-attachment jazz.

One month into this particular India trip, I'd been heavily berating myself for all the mental sludge and turmoil I'd been slogging through on the road. Sure, there were the daily physical hardships and hassles— the discomforts, bellyaches, and valid reasons to gripe. But this was a deeper despair. By the time Tim and I got to Lucknow, I was a downright Negative Nelly, having lost my Perky Pollyanna ways somewhere back in holy Rishikesh.

Lucknow was a testing ground for me, due to the very fact that we were visiting the home of one of Tim's spiritual teachers—his grand-guru Sri H.W.L. Poonja, known as "Papaji." Papaji himself was a student of one of India's most beloved saints of the early 20th century—Ramana Maharshi, sage of Arunachala, in Tiruvannamalai, Tamil Nadu, South India.

During the 1980s and into the 1990s, Papaji was a great disseminator of the Advaita teachings of self-inquiry and Ultimate Awareness, sharing the teachings of Ramana and "Who Am I?" as well as inspiring contemporary Western teachers of self-realization such as Mooji, Gangaji, and Eli Jaxon-Bear, who is Tim's direct teacher in the U.S.

Papaji passed away in his Lucknow home in 1997. Tim wanted to visit and pay respects to his teacher's teacher and soak up the darshan. I agreed to support him and went along for the ride—to learn, inquire, and see what was there for myself.

We were welcomed into a beautiful homestay outside the Lucknow city center, situated next door to the *Satsang Bhavan* (spiritual teaching building). The homestay included the most comfortable surroundings I've yet to experience in India: organic food, a happy staff, Internet in the room, A/C... even a washing machine at our disposal! At the guru's, life was easy and comfortable.

Soon after our arrival, however, my internal rumblings and mental misery multiplied, and even the washing machine couldn't launder my blues away.

I was not happy there, in guru-land. I have always experienced a wide range of feelings when it comes to "The Guru Question." My reactionary human nature rises up and rears its ugly head toward the roles played by both teacher and student. Sometimes, I feel anger; at other times, confusion at not having experienced some semblance of ecstatic state of divine union through the grace of the guru.

My questioning nature arises: Why is one person "chosen" to have bliss bestowed upon them through a meeting with a guru, thus experiencing states of *samadhi* (calmness and unity with the Divine), *shaktipat* (the transmission of spiritual energy from one individual to another), and such and such, while another pilgrim or seeker (i.e., myself) continues to trudge along, wading through day-to-day challenges—with no WHAMMY-O! fall-in-love oohs and aahs, no swooning blissful bhakti union with a true teacher, enlightened master, or realized being?

In Lucknow, try as I might to feel the love, I instead stewed inside over "The Guru Question," directing a lot of it toward Tim, who was quite comfortable having a Teacher with a capital T.

My own mind was running tapes. A guru: to have or have not? Why didn't I get one, too? Can I get along with a partner who has a guru? Why do I care, anyway? Is this all for the birds? Maybe I should fly home and get a real job, for cryin' out loud. And, who the hell cares, anyway?

My skin crawled as I felt a mixture of frustration and boredom. I wanted to tell the devotees, with their pictures of Papaji plastered all over every room's walls, to take a flying leap into their own special sea of bliss, their Truth, their One Heart, their Self-Realization.

My inner tension had been spilling over into my relations with Tim. His joy at being in the surroundings of this guru was only serving to piss me off even more. Tim's serenity and subtle smile only served to make my lack of ease more apparent, agitated, amped.

I wanted to change my vibration—I did, I did! I wanted to understand. I wanted to let go of judgment. I had been reading the books, talking with others, staring at the portraits placed on every wall. What to do?

I'd decided to give it all a chance—see if I could bust through my barriers.

And then one day during my brief stay, we made a special visit to the actual family home of Papaji to pay respect to his mahasamadhi resting place.

At the middle-class Poonja home, we were warmly greeted by Papaji's daughter-in-law, Usha. After a brief conversation, Tim and I were ushered into the guru's very own bedroom, which had been left exactly as it was upon his death. Papaji's personal items were left just so—the calendar on the wall marking his passing, his sandals, his personal altar and dried flower wreaths, incense, and candles.

The small bedroom was so humble, so real, so inviting. His presence was deep and the energy intense. I was touched.

We were left alone in the room as long as we wanted. My own intention was to offer gratitude for this highly respected teacher's grace in having me there, finicky and resistant as I was, as well as to receive some of the darshan emanating from the personal chambers of a self-realized master. It had been exactly ten years since Papaji left his body to take mahasamadhi, but the sweetness and stillness were completely palpable.

Tim and I sat cross-legged, on the floor and facing each other, to meditate a few minutes. We each closed our eyes and went within, to our respective inner abodes. My monkey mind began performing its usual gymnastics, so I first tried to quiet and concentrate the mind by practicing *anapana* awareness meditation, observing the breath.

But after a minute, seated on the floor next to this guru's very own bed, amongst his personal items, I realized I'd rather take this rare opportunity to have a direct "Conversation with Papaji"—to get clear on a few things, one-on-one. *Since consciousness is a constant, independent of a physical body*, I thought, *there should be no reason why this Teacher and I can't have a real-time rap.*

"Papaji," I began the exchange silently, "I'm suffering so very much and am very angry about this whole enlightenment-guru-master gig. I don't get *It*, whatever *It* is. Sometimes, I feel my suffering has *increased* with awareness, instead of getting relief. Can you help me?" I continued, "I am praying for relief so that I can be freed from self-centeredness and be of service to others. I'm no good to anyone else if I'm so tied up in knots of anger and judgment about this whole thing."

I heard his reply, a warm and deep voice in my mind, which made my heart seize up and a lump rise in my throat.

"Erin, the sign of a true master is not freedom from suffering. It is that you continue to go on, even in the midst of pain. That you haven't given up, that you stay AWARE, conscious and alert of your state, even amidst the pain, as well as the joy. That you even TRY to bring goodwill, happiness, and joy to others, to alleviate the suffering of others, even while you suffer still. You keep on keeping on, in spite of your personal pain—you make the effort, and you keep standing tall. Don't worry about getting *It*, because that IS the point: There is Nothing to get. You already have *It*."

A few big tears rolled down my cheeks, and I felt my heart open like a lotus blossom. Sweet relief! There was no big thing, no big deal, no "transmission" that I wasn't lucky enough, good enough, or "dharma-fied" enough to get. Because I already had *It*, and *It* is absolutely Nothing! The truth is so paradoxical and strange.

After our time in meditation, Usha served us chai and sweets in the living room. An intelligent, well-educated Indian woman, Usha is a retired head of a social work government agency, who now stays home to take care of grandchildren and keep things in order.

Between sips of chai, while flipping through dozens upon dozens of Papaji's family photo albums, Tim and I chitchatted with Usha.

I had lots of questions.

With all these thousands of Westerners streaming into Lucknow for two decades to learn from her father-in-law, this self-realized master, I asked Usha what it was like to be with Papaji. I wanted to know if she was personally experiencing a special bliss, this "fully awake" heart consciousness that devotees speak of—since she was living in the same house with the guru himself. I wanted to know if she was enlightened, liberated, free.

I got the feeling she'd been asked this question before. Like a true teacher herself, she chose to answer the question indirectly by telling a simple story. In a cheerful, matter-of-fact manner, she explained:

"Papaji was a very loving father-in-law. He made me free by taking care of my baby son—his grandson—during the day, when I wanted to go back to work for my career. That is how he made me free."

Usha's answer reminded me that true freedom can be much more straightforward than blissful states and ecstatic union. She continued, and I noticed a tiny glimmer of personal pride shining through—just a hint.

"And Papaji always said to me that I made him free. I kept the house, I made the meals, I took care of him so that he didn't have to think about these things, so he could spend time teaching his students. In this way, he said, I made *him* free."

> *Before enlightenment: chop wood, carry water.*
> *After enlightenment: chop wood, carry water.*
> ~ *Zen proverb*

At the Cremation Grounds
Varanasi
October 31, 2007
Earth to earth, ashes to ashes, dust to dust.
In sure and certain hope of the Resurrection into eternal life.
~ Book of Common Prayer

Happy Halloween. We are in Varanasi, also known as Benares.

In stark contrast to her headwaters near Rishikesh, where the river is relatively clean and pure, often turquoise in color, here in Varanasi, the Ganges is filthy, foul, and filled with death.

Yes, death.

Idly strolling along the riverbank *ghats*—the steps leading to the water—Tim and I are stopped in our tracks by an awesome spectacle, a peculiar and powerful sight vastly unfamiliar to Western eyes. We are at Harischandra (Moon of Vishnu) Ghat, and there are three funeral pyres flaming away directly before us.

In keeping with the shadow, spook, and spirit of Samhain (the Celtic New Year also known as All Hallow's Eve), I tell Tim I can't think of a better way to spend the day than exploring the burning ghats of Benares on the banks of the Ganges.

It is actually a peaceful place. We make our way to a bench and seat ourselves amongst the males of the departed's family.

Looking down into the largest bonfire, we try to ascertain whether we can see the corpse. Indeed, we see the head, with hair disappearing as the flames dance around the body.

This is the playing field of Shiva and Kali, in their roles of wrathful god and goddess. This is the bridge, the portal to the other side. It's broad daylight, which is a good thing, as the energies arising from this point are pulsing and throbbing. I don't think I would be hanging out here long without a male companion. In fact, amongst the throngs, I am the only female.

Tim and I are respectfully viewing the cremation, observing the scene. "I wonder how long it takes for the body to completely burn," Tim whispers to me.

Softly I reply, "I think it has to burn until the skull completely explodes."

From out of nowhere, a very dark and dignified Indian has seated himself next to Tim's right side. "It takes about three hours," the stranger states in perfect English, surprising us with his observation of our discussion. We had no idea we were being observed. The man introduces himself as Mr. Choudry, the family who oversees Harischandra Ghat's activities. Over the next hour, he proceeds to explain to us the ins and outs of life overseeing the funeral pyres.

Mr. Choudry ("Choudri*ji*," indicating respect) takes great pride in his profession.

When I look at this pitch-dark Indian man, I see Kali herself, in the form of Smasana, the wrathful goddess in her element: the cremation grounds. I realize that on this Halloween day, Tim and I are fortunate enough to come face to face with a very intimate friend of the Grim Reaper himself: He Who Deals in Death.

Mr. Choudry's eyes are red-rimmed, from smoke or burnout, or both. His teeth are black and chipped with gaps and holes, completely ruined from his self-professed fifty-paan-a-day chewing habit. His lips are permanently stained from the blood-red betelnut.

His skin is black as coal. He's got a silver serpent ring coiled around his left ring finger, wedded to Shiva. He's married to his profession as a dealer of death, and he's happy, whole, and honored to be providing the world with one of the most important duties: liberation of the soul from the physical realm.

Mr. Choudry explains to us that his family is one of the most important, well-respected families in Varanasi—in fact, in all of India. The Choudry family has been burning bodies and assisting souls to reach *moksha* (liberation) for forty-five generations over thirty centuries.

Tim and I know there's going to be a catch after we're through talking this man's ear off. We've been warned of this particular scheme, and so we know there's a punch line at the end. Isn't there always a price to pay when bantering with the boatman of the River Styx? We'll surely be asked to donate rupees for firewood (the scarcest of resources in the dry plains of southern Uttar Pradesh) so that the poorest of Indians can afford to have their brethren burned in Benares. Yet, this upcoming catch doesn't deter us; we're enraptured with Choudriji's explanation of the cremation process. "Please continue," we encourage.

Choudry: "Yes, it takes about three hours to burn fully before the ashes are offered to the holy Ganga. The body needs to be washed in the river by a male relative; this man also bathes in the river first, and he must be wearing all white. The man then walks around the body five times before the fire is lit. Five is the number of elements in our Hindu religion: earth, sky, fire, water, and ether.

"There are six classes of humans that will not be cremated: those dying from smallpox; those who die from a snake bite; lepers with no legs and no hands; children under the age of nine; a pregnant woman; and holy sadhus, or babas. This is because these people are already considered purified and have no need for the holy fires. In these cases, the bodies are tied to a heavy stone, taken to the middle of Ganga, and dropped directly into the river.

"There are three pyres here: one for the average Indian, one for the poor—the wood is acquired through donation—and one for the rich.

"At my ghat, Harischandra, anyone can be cremated—Hindus, Christians, all castes. Eighteen Europeans have been burned here. At the other main burning ghat, Manikarnika, only Hindus may be burned."

Tim and I look at each other. I know we are both wondering whether being given to the Ganga at life's end would be a desirable way to pass over. We raise our eyebrows in a look that says "possible," and return to listening intently to our discourse on death.

Choudry continues: "The ideal is for the soul to be released entirely from the worldly plane and attain moksha—liberation. All is burned except for one part of the body. For a man, the chest flesh is salvaged. For a woman, the flesh of the hips is saved from the flames. The reason is that this part of the body contains the karma of the man or woman. This flesh is offered to the river, to the fishes. The fish eat the flesh—the chest or hips—and then communicate to the God, telling God whether the person has enough good karma to move on to nirvana, avoiding rebirth evermore. If the person is not ready to attain full liberation, the fish tell God, and the person is then reborn into the world as a dog, camel, monkey, fish—any animal—or again, as a person, so as to work out in another lifetime their own salvation and meet their karma. This is the role of the fishes."

Tim comments that the smoke from the pyres is wafting heavily all around us, yet oddly, it is not offensive, and the ash is mild. "It is the blessing of Lord Shiva that there is never any foul smell from the fires. Every single fire, which we call *agni*, comes from coals of our family holy fire, the *dhuni*, which has been kept burning for forty-five generations."

A new body—that of a young man—is being carried with a family procession into the river. The corpse is draped in white and wearing garland upon garland of marigolds. We watch in solemnity, with respectful interest.

After the body is bathed, a huddle of male family members escorts the father of the dead son to the seat next to ours. He is broken, doing everything he can not to cry. But, even if tears do not fall from his eyes, he is wailing in agony. Choudry tells a worker to get the man some *paani* (water) to calm the grieving father.

Looking around, it is clear I am the only female observing the ceremony. The male family members are looking on at the current cremation pyre. Choudry explains, "No women are to come to the ceremony. This is because the soul must be free to go, and if woman is crying, crying—then the soul will not be free to liberate itself from the body and earthly plane. So, no female family members must come."

There is a body draped in a cloth perched on a concrete slab nearby, and Tim inquires as to when it would be burned. "The family is on its way from Bombay," says Choudry. "They should be here tonight. The body must wait until family is here. We are a twenty-four-hour operation, burning constantly."

It sounds like he's talking about an In-N-Out Burger drive-through, and I hide a smile.

"In fact, we could burn more bodies here. Some years back, the Indian government installed this building over here, to my right, with electric incinerators. The Indians tried this out for a few years, but never got used to it. They all want the real thing—the wood and traditional method.

"Some families cannot afford the right amount of wood. Five or ten years before, the poor families would use only twenty or thirty kilograms, but then we had problems in Varanasi: you would see an arm, or a leg, or half-burned corpse floating down the river because it was not burned properly. We need over three hundred and fifty kilograms of wood to fully burn a body." *That's a lot of wood*, I'm thinking. "For the poor families, they pay what they can. We also sift through the ashes of the rich-people pyres and use the jewelry and ornaments of those families to buy wood for the poor burnings."

True to the guidebook, Choudry is going in for the request for rupees, appealing to our compassion and sensitivity to buy wood for the poor. Tim looks at me and mouths, "LP." I immediately get what he's trying to say: it's our private code for the *Lonely Planet* guidebook warning for scams—meaning, here comes the catch.

And the catch it came, so smooth and subtle, one would almost not know it was delivered:

"So, if you like—of course, no pressure—if you find it in your hearts to make a small donation for the poor family firewood, it would be gladly accepted."

I'm quick to respond, not sure how I feel about contributing on the spot. "Thank you very much, Mr. Choudry. We very much appreciate your time and your position—you have a very important job, and you are very lucky. This has been a gift, all of this explanation, and we will consider your request. But we will not donate today—only after we have discussed it amongst ourselves, then we will return with our contribution."

"No problem, no problem," Choudry replies. He's a smooth talker, and well-practiced, probably working this deal several times a day with soft-hearted Western tourists. Whether or not he is actually a forty-fifth-generation member of the Varanasi Choudry Family or just a hustler, Tim and I concur later that his help and teaching do deserve a small tip; hopefully, the funds will indeed find their way to assist the poorer families, but it may just land in the Death Dealer's pockets, which is okay, too. I'm also quite aware that the gods do appreciate small sacrifices on the part of us humans, and since this is the stomping ground of the cosmic badasses Shiva and Kali, I'm not about to act blasé or disrespectful in any way.

At the end of our acquaintance, after the sun has long dropped below the horizon, we are personally escorted behind the pyres to a small, secret Kali *mandir* belonging to the Choudry family.

It is dark now, and the riverfront ghat area is suddenly made even darker as there is a power cut and blackout. It is customary but unpredictable, occurring two to three times daily in Varanasi. Tim and I hasten to follow behind Choudriji in the darkness, attempting to sidestep ashes and muck and mire in the process.

Having reached the small Kali temple, Mr. Choudry opens up the red, steel-barred doors that enclose and protect the deity. "There She is," he says, and, just for a brief second, he flashes his dim torch on her naked, black body.

I barely catch a glimpse of her lolling, red tongue and bow my head in respect before he's turned off the flashlight and it is pitch-black dark again. Choudry swiftly instructs, "Close the gates." I quickly obey, and Tim and I are escorted back to the burning grounds to find our way home in the dark.

We both agree it's been a perfect way to spend All Hallow's Eve.

As the pagans believe, the crack between worlds—the veil between life and death—is lifted at Halloween. In fact, it is as if the gods have created for us our very own lesson in the shadowy side this evening: reminders that all is impermanent, death is a part of life, and each and every one of us shares the same fate.

All the more reason to enjoy, enjoy, enjoy the life!

> *For certain is death for the born*
> *And certain is birth for the dead;*
> *Therefore over the inevitable*
> *Thou shouldst not grieve.*
> *- Bhagavad Gita*

Afterword: Please Allow Me to Introduce Myself

If the Fab Four represent the sweetness and enlightenment that is Rishikesh, then Varanasi, in contrast, would belong to those shadowy brother Brits known for more raunchiness with their rock—the Rolling Stones.

Even though there can be nothing remotely related to evil in the energy of the burning ghats (in contrast; it is a place of liberation), with the tone of Halloween at hand, I must say that meeting Mr. Choudry reminds me of "Sympathy for the Devil," that sinister, saucy Stones tribute to Lucifer himself...

Let me please introduce myself
I'm a man of wealth and taste
And I laid traps for troubadours
Who get killed before they reached Bombay

It is a little-known fact that the Rolling Stones Records label—that of the red lips and lolling tongue—was indeed chosen by the band as a symbol of the merciless, yet ever merciful, goddess Kali. Most would deduce that it represents the ample mouth and lips of Mick Jagger, but that's not the case. It is an icon of the Mother Kali Herself. Jai Maa.

The Abode of the Snake King
Bodh Gaya
November 8, 2007

Our next tale hails from Bodh Gaya, home of the Buddha's full enlightenment under the protective covering of the Bodhi Tree in approximately 500 B.C.

Bodh Gaya is considered the most important of all Buddhist pilgrimage sites, the others being Lumbini (Nepal), the birthplace of Buddha; Sarnath (near Varanasi), where he delivered his first sermon on the Four Noble Truths in Deer Park; and Kushinagar (near the Nepalese border), the place of Buddha's death and cremation.

It is in Bodh Gaya that I came to understand a smidgen of Buddha's Second Noble Truth more fully.

The causes of suffering are craving and desire.

As many of my most potent life lessons play out, this direct experience of the divine occurred unexpectedly, with the guidance of Mother Nature...

After an exhausting sixteen-hour haul from Kushinagar, Tim and I rolled into Bodh Gaya, the holiest place of Buddhism, ironically situated in the poorest, least-literate state in the nation, Bihar.

It was late in the evening upon our arrival to the small pilgrimage town. We took a room at the first decent guest house on our path. I slept like a stone Buddhist *stupa*, plain beat from the hard day's journey. The air was getting crisp, and November's cooling currents enabled a deeper sleep.

Next morn, I awoke with a vivid dream fresh in my mind, which I immediately relayed to Tim.

"I dreamt of a large Buddha statue in the middle of a pond of sorts. The Buddha was gilded and finely detailed, and I was surprised to see it erected in the middle of a pool of filthy water, filled with garbage and decomposing matter. The Buddha was inaccessible through the sludge."

We weren't sure what the dream meant; I mused that it may have been reflective of our shared feelings about how sacred shrines and pilgrimage points seem so disrespected in India, surrounded by so much decay, garbage, greed, and hassle.

Moving on from the dream and entering waking life, Tim and I geared up and set out to explore the Mahabodhi Temple—the main focal point of Bodh Gaya and ultimate destination of Buddhist pilgrims worldwide.

The huge Mahabodhi complex was divine, peaceful, and—we were pleased to find—protected from the hustle, bustle, pollution, and chaos of the India lying just a stone's throw outside the gates.

In the center of the Mahabodhi complex grows a huge offspring of the original Bodhi Tree—a sapling having been protected and preserved in Sri Lanka while Buddhism went through its own version of the Dark Ages in its Indian birthplace.

The infamous Bodhi Tree is said to be the exact point on Earth that Buddha sat in meditation with *adhitthana*—strong determination—and came to fully realize the nature of suffering and the path to liberation.

Upon entering the Mahabodhi complex, Tim and I circumambulated the main shrine three times clockwise in honor of the Triple Gem, symbolically taking refuge in Buddha, Dharma, and Sangha.

Next, we paused to sit with two elderly Tibetans—one monk and one nun—who were chanting nonstop *om mane padme hum* mantras, counting off on their beaded malas. I reveled in soaking up the good energy of these *bhikkhus*, marveling at how effortless it was to drop into meditation in close proximity to incredibly dedicated Dharma practitioners.

After some time, Tim and I decided to circumnavigate the entire temple complex and explore the outlying gardens on our own. At the far east corner of the grounds, we saw a large body of water peeking through the trees and stone pillars.

"Let's go check it out. It looks like a lake," I said.

A lake it was. It was Mucalinda Lake, and a large, gilded Buddha, inaccessible without a boat, was perched directly in the middle—just like in my dream the night before.

We read the sign, which explained Mother Nature's role here during the sixth week of Buddha's enlightenment process.

MUCALINDA LAKE
The Abode of the Snake King
Lord Buddha spent the sixth week in meditation here.
While he was meditating, severe thunderstorm broke out.
To protect him from the violent wind and rain even the creatures came
out for his safety.

"Ah, so the serpent that's crowning the Buddha on the statue must be the Snake King that protected him during the storm," I said.

Tim pulled out the information pamphlet he had picked up on the way into the Complex. The pamphlet confirmed that, yes, the colorful, hooded cobra king had risen from the bottom of the lake during the storm to protect Buddha from the elements so that he could continue his contemplation on Truth, undisturbed.

We walked down the steps leading to the water, and, suddenly, we noticed the water was rippling—moving. Slowly at first, then with greater and greater turbidity. It was as if raindrops from the powerful storm 2,500 years ago were still falling.

Then we saw, just below us, thrashing around and causing the splashing and disruption, thousands upon thousands of humongous, eerie-looking catfish.

These were no ordinary New Orleans-style catfish. These were *something-wicked-this-way-comes-out-of-a-cesspool* fish—two feet long with four-inch wide, gaping orifices. Creatures with long antenna-like protuberances stemming from their huge round mouths. Black and slimy, sucking the garbage and filth from the sides of the ghat steps leading into the lake.

At first sight, all I could think was how disgusting these fish were, slithering around the golden Buddha. Yet it quickly dawned on me that these slimy sea sentinels were helpers, protecting Siddhartha from anyone stepping foot or swimming near him in any way.

"Oh my god, Tim, it's the lake from my dream. Look how the filth and sludge are surrounding the Buddha, keeping him safe." No one would dare enter that lake willingly. Clearly, these fish were still, 2,500 years later, playing the role of protecting the Enlightened One.

But the Abode of the Snake King held a lesson more significant than the nature of duality and the contrasts of purity and filth. Standing there watching with disgust, these fishy friends, desperately gasping for a tiny morsel of detritus, gave me a glimpse into the true nature of Desire.

These thousands of creepy creatures, endlessly flopping on top of each other, reminded me of the human experience. When we are acting unconsciously, how are we any different than these fish? We flop around, flailing, falling over ourselves and on top of each other, clinging and craving to have our desires fulfilled, with no end to the struggle until we realize the futility of the grasping and groping.

Lifetime after lifetime, until we wake up, there is nothing underneath each desire, except the rising up of yet another desire. Perhaps we get the top-paying job, only to realize that wasn't quite "it." We have the hot love affair with the sexy coworker, and that's not the end to it either.

We gorge ourselves with hot crème brûlée, finish off another bottle of wine, go see the pyramids of Giza, buy the convertible BMW—and somehow, there is still… dissatisfaction.

Tim and I pondered this for a while, watching the chaos of splashing fish beneath our feet. We were horrified and happy at the same time. The fish were giving us such insight in the very best way—unsolicited and spontaneous.

While we sat, a maroon-robed Tibetan monk strolled up to the concrete platform overlooking the lake. He had a bag of dried bread, and he began throwing the breadcrumbs out to the fish.

The fish went wild, literally leaping and flying through the air and clamoring up the sides of the concrete walls to manage a morsel. Huge fish lips stretched wide open, gaping with cavernous, desperate mouths, aching to catch one tiny crumb.

Now, perhaps the monk was simply bored, throwing out leftover scraps to the scavengers. Or perhaps he was choosing to help his animal brethren, with compassion for all living beings, like a good and true Buddhist.

Or, perhaps he was consciously helping each little fish soul to fulfill one more desire. In my imagination, I heard the monk's sentiment:

"Eat, eat, my fishy friends. See that there is no end to the craving. It matters not whether you are a top politician, movie star, peasant, or scum-sucking catfish living in the middle of a putrid lake in the poorest state in India. The nature of desire is the same. So eat, eat, my fishy friends! Have your desires fulfilled, each and every one! And come to realize that there is no end to desire."

How bizarre; how very, very bizarre. But! The next time I'm stuck in the muck, wanting things to be different than they are—craving this impermanent pleasure, avoiding that passing pain—maybe I'll grovel and grope for fulfillment, one more time…

Or maybe I'll remember those fish. Observe the desire. The wanting. The ache…

And let it pass…

Without getting hooked.

"You Have to Be Willing to Die"
Kolkata (Calcutta)
November 18, 2007

After six months of time with Tim, I was clear on one thing: suffering. My own.

Pain I was vastly familiar with—psychological pain even—and I knew from years of meditation, yoga, spiritual development, and "working on myself" that pain is a part of life and that the Buddha taught that "enlightenment is the end of suffering."

I WAS clearly still suffering, especially from excruciating perfectionism. POOR GIRL. So much self; so much "me, me, me" to hate, to judge, to beat up!

Once again, I had to admit defeat. He was going to fly to Chennai solo and travel onward to the holy mountain of Tiruvannamalai. I would stay behind in Kolkata to sort my own head out. I was in no shape to be in partnership with anyone, let alone Tim, no matter how spiritual he may be.

Being with Tim drove me crazy because, although his maturity was less developed than mine, he had PEACE OF MIND. He was totally okay with "What Is," no matter what! He had awakened, so to speak, and knew that everything was the play of consciousness. That damned peace was there, no matter what. He may get sick or scared or angry, but there was an underlying resting that he was seated in, within and through it all. Tim was seated in the Self, with a capital S.

The last night in Kolkata, just before he left, I made him go with me to the one watering hole in the backpacking district. I ordered a watered-down Indian vodka drink called a "White Mischief." Tim ordered club soda. Sipping the tasteless cocktail, I humbled myself before Tim. I was crying, totally miserable. I'd called off the Search, as Papaji had told me, and I'd given up *trying* to be free from existential suffering. And I was clearly ready. My inner life sucked. It was great on the outside—lots to be grateful for—but on the inside, self-hatred was rampant, like a cancer. Clearly, there was nothing more I could do!

Yet, there were two things left:

1. To ask for help

2. To be done with it ALL.

I had prayed with all of my heart that if I was meant to receive a real Teacher in this life, one that I could fully trust and surrender to, that he or she be revealed to me.

"Tim, I can't do it. I need help," I said to him.

He repeated two things he'd been telling me from Day One of meeting each other, only this time I got it:

1. You have to be willing to die. You have to be ready to die.

2. You have to want Awakening (Truth, Enlightenment, Realization) more than anything else. You have to put everything you have, every-thing in your entire life, into this, in your heart. In fact, Truth has to be the ONLY thing you desire. And then, paradoxically, you gotta let that all go!

And then Tim reminded me of the irony that there is nothing, noth-ing at all, that one can *do* to cause an awakening to happen.

We let go entirely… and… then… we see…

The next morning, Tim took a taxi to the airport to fly to Chennai without me. I at least felt some relief that I could suffer on my own, even though my heart was broken. *Another failed relationship*, I told myself. *I'll just keep moving forward, alone. Been here before.*

I spent a couple more days in Kolkata, doing my best to soak up the magic of Kali's city. Cold comfort tooling around the City of Joy.

"Fuck it," I said to myself. "If there's nothing more to do, if there's no way I can help myself get out of this suffering, I quit this spiritual India mumbo jumbo traveling. I'm done. I'm going to fly to Goa to party at the beach."

Kicked Out of Kali's Nest
Kolkata (Calcutta)
November 21, 2007

It's a Wednesday morning, November 21, the eve of the American Thanksgiving, as I ready myself to take off once again after a week's stay in The City of Joy.

Begrudgingly, I load up my pack, sad to say goodbye to this grand metropolis, lush with history and romance, poetry, and political activism—and the omnipresence of Kali, the city's patron deity.

I'm feeling the ache that comes when one leaves a lover, unsure of whether it's the last time or a "'til the next time."

Opting for the latter, I present a small token of my affection to the live-in employees of the Salvation Army Red Shield Guest House as a way to show them—and me—that I'll be back.

I've bought them a scarlet-colored potted plant—a Dracaena, "dragon's blood"—for their garden, in remembrance of the good army's Guest House—indeed the iconic travelers' guest house on Sudder Street, aka Backpacker Central. I think Little Orphan Annie and I would agree: what it lacks in comfort, the Salvation Army makes up in character. Ancient and quirky make a great mix, even when the staircase is literally tied to a wall beam with a frayed rope to keep the entire structure from sliding down and caving in.

"It's lovely! We keep it here for you to come and visit," the middle-aged, Christian cleaning lady proclaims, holding up my potted plant offering and motioning to the corner of the courtyard where the sun shines longest. She shuffles off in her gray-with-red-trim sari uniform and places the red snake plant in its new home.

I watch her, happy with my choice to buy the workers a gift, and happy that a piece of my heart gets to stay in Kali's own city, even if I am off to play nomad.

The taxi-wallah is waiting for me, holding the trunk open, diesel engine idling and hiccupping substantial plumes of black smoke into the courtyard. As the driver tosses my bag in the boot, I savor the picture. My favorite taxi: the banana-yellow, Ambassador cab with 1940's vintage flair. In Kolkata, I always feel to be in a mixture of New York City and colonial British India—and, like shoes make the outfit, here it's the yellow Ambassadors with their classic curves and ample size that make the city.

Our cab drives off toward the northern suburb of Dum Dum, where the Kolkata Airport is, and I daydream and wonder what it would be like to live there and tell people I live in Dum Dum. After we get stuck in a very polluted, very hot, and very honky traffic jam for a full fifteen motionless minutes, I decide that I'd rather live anywhere else than Dum Dum.

Soon, I tell myself as I dig through my day bag to pull out my e-ticket to Goa, *you'll be in paradise…*

"Thank God," I mutter to myself as we arrive at the airport terminus thirty minutes later than planned. I hop out of the cab and hand over two hundred rupees and a twenty-rupee tip to the driver—bargaining done in advance, as usual—as he plops my pack on the curb.

"Happy Journey Goa!" the driver waves as he sputters off in the Ambassador.

Yes, Goa. Beaches, papaya, sunsets… and rest for my weary body. I need a holiday.

As I enter the Departure terminal, I get the feeling that something is awry, yet I can't quite put my finger on it. I often get anxious or antsy when I'm about to board a long-distance Indian train and head off into unknown horizons, even when I know I'll be perfectly fine. But this unsettledness was decidedly different. I've never flown domestically in India.

I immediately start giving myself undue, unnecessary criticism for choosing to fly across the nation, from the northeast corner to the southwest coast of the country, in one fell swoop. Traversing the Indian subcontinent diagonally, for ten times the cost of a train, would take four hours and $120, versus forty hours and twelve bucks by train. In other words, a massive face-off of time versus money.

Since I have heaps of time, and I actually enjoy second-class Indian train travel—the people, the scenery, the chance to catch up on reading, and the gradual entry into a new region and microclimate—I am mentally kicking myself that I caved in to the temptation to fly.

Why? Why did I choose to fly? I am asking myself. Ah yes, the flight sounds delightfully cozy and comfy in theory, and I can afford it. Still, suddenly, I realize I'm feeling funny about flying… because *it's domestic Indian air travel*!

It's one thing to have crazed, unruly, disorganized disruption in the railway terminus, at the bus stands, even on the national highways. ("The other day while I was driving along a pothole my car fell into a road," quipped *Times of India* columnist Jug Suraiya.)

But coming face to face with such unnerved feelings of madness when you're about to launch yourself thirty thousand feet into the potentially not-so-friendly skies—that's another story entirely. Suddenly, I'm finding it hard to stomach being at the mercy of managers, pilots, and flight attendants who are the actual embodiment of typical, intranational Indian chaos.

At the check-in queue for the latest and greatest, "cheap and best" domestic airline, I'm cast about like a bumper car between lines of streaming travelers. I'm like a hamster on a wheel, never making progress. Get to one counter, I'm told to move to the next. Get to the front of the next counter, and I'm told that the original counter is the correct one.

It's bad. I'm already frazzled, and the Indians appear worse off than me—they're *hyper* and frazzled. I'm thrust amidst pushing throngs of Indians who are shouting for no reason at all.

As I spontaneously begin to practice *anapana* meditation, watching my breath to take my mind off my frayed nerves, I come to the immediate, absolute truism that airports (specifically, *airplanes*) and hyper Indians are a bad combination. Period.

The ticket hostess at the check-in counter screams orders right and left, tossing destination luggage tags through the air, which the lone baggage handler scrambles to catch and stick on the correct bag before he falls behind her pace and the bags disappear beyond the conveyer belt portal without tags.

The testy hostess (*Prithi*... I check her nametag, ostensibly in case I need to report my own death-by-flight accident) is simultaneously tap-tap-tapping her keyboard, checking people in, and shouting out seat availability to the complaining Indians—who are all upper-middle (or upper) class, with comparably uppity attitudes.

Meanwhile, Miss Prithi, who didn't pass the course training sections on Patience, Proper Multitasking, or Pleasantries, barks orders into a walkie-talkie held in her left hand while she continues to tap-tap-tap the keyboard and check folks in with her right hand—except when her cell phone rings and she tag-teams it: the left ear on the cell, the right ear listening to the radio.

While one authority gives orders on the mobile—is that her personal phone?—I watch the instructions pass through the synapses in her brain, after which she yells them back out into the walkie-talkie. My Bengali is worse than my Hindi. It is, frankly, nil, so I can't tell what she's shouting, except for something about "airstrip" and "takeoff."

Oh my God. If we all lift off in the first place, I hope to God the pilots are less frenetic up there.

My face morphs into an inadvertent scowl. *I wish, oh, how I wish I'd toughed out the three-day train trip instead!*

I try to forget about the not one but two near-miss takeoff incidents I'd read about in yesterday's local paper as I—*Finally!*—catch a glimpse of a boarding pass being thrust toward me from the hectic hostess' outstretched hand. It's a hand extended all the way over the heads of at least four Indians to reach me, since there's no such thing as "one at a time" in an Indian queue—even if it is an airport. Not a chance.

I snatch the golden pass from Miss Prithi's paw and make to haul off to the gate, but not without taking a third glance to ensure that my bag was indeed tagged "Goa" by the baggage handler, who looks as if he's had just about enough of it all himself—tossed tags fluttering in his face, trying to keep it all together while passengers and Prithi bark back and forth. Madness.

Hang in there, buddy. I'm right there with you. Just get that there big blue backpack on the conveyer belt without a mix-up, and then you can go have yourself a nice long chai break.

Times like these, I attempt to console myself with, *It could be worse.*

This time, however, I think, *I don't even want to know what any worse could look like.* I step on to the mini-shuttle that will taxi us to the boarding zone. *At this point, it's out of my control.*

"Better Than Starving"
Kolkata Airport
November 21, 2007

Yes, it's out of my control.

And, at this point, I am officially worried.

I've got the feeling that something isn't going to go down exactly as planned on this particular flight.

A buttoned-up, sophisticated-looking Indian man is rudely making a scene with the airline employees at the gate. It's fifteen minutes past our boarding time, and he demands to know why we can't board the plane.

Standing in line with the rest of the passengers, I look around and notice that the bulk of the lot represents a class of people that I'm less familiar with in India. They seem to be *nouveau rich* Indians—those privileged few who are up and coming with the new economy. They have a sense of entitlement, which gives me a bad taste in my mouth. I hate it. I hate the attitude of "I deserve to be served," a way of looking down at others, though I've surely been unconsciously guilty of the same at some point. I'm not used to traveling with this segment of the population. This whole domestic Indian air travel get-up is a new experience for me entirely.

Half an hour later, we are allowed to board the plane—spiffy and sparkling clean, a brand-new Boeing for India's latest discount domestic carrier—and I find I'm seated next to a sour-faced businessman. I sit down and place my handbag near my feet while I get myself organized.

"You can't put your bag there," he says to me. "It's not allowed."

I look at him, flatly, without saying a thing, and push the handbag under the seat in front of me.

Everybody on this flight—myself now included—seems to have their panties in a wad. It's now forty-five minutes past our scheduled take-off. The Muzak track at high volume has looped itself around for the umpteenth time, and I can't take much more of the tinny songs that are designed to be calming, but clearly have the opposite effect.

The flight attendants keep repeating the mantra, "We are waiting to be cleared for takeoff. Please be patient. We are waiting to be cleared for takeoff. Please be patient."

One hour later—the cabin unbearably stuffy due to canned-air vents on full blast that actually seem to be exuding heat on a sticky hot day, passengers shifting uncomfortably in their strapped-in positions—we're still not moving. I'm afraid there's going to be a mutiny. Not only that, I'm starving. I was waiting to buy some sort of in-flight SnakPak once the plane took off—the bananas and packets of dried mung dal ran out a long time ago, and I've got that unnerving, hypoglycemic wave of disorientation. I push the little signal-light button that brings an attendant to my seat.

"Excuse me. I know we're waiting for takeoff, but I... I'm really, really hungry, and I was just wondering if you might have some nuts or some other snack to eat?" I ask the attendant politely.

"No, I'm sorry, but I can *sell* you some biscuits," she replies.

Biscuits? *Cookies!* Now I'm stuck. For the past three years, I haven't been eating sugar—any at all—in order to sort my sensitive system out of the "sugar blues" cycle, and all that's on board at this moment are cookies?

But I'm *starving.*

Like a movie in my head, I flash back to a brief exchange I'd had the year prior with an American renunciate friend: Baba Jay, originally from

L.A., who regularly buys ten-cent packets of sugar biscuits to feed to the stray dogs wherever he goes. The sick and mangy hounds scarf down the cookies with great gusto and trot off with their heads held just a little bit higher, one more day to live.

"Isn't sugar supposed to be bad for dogs?" I once asked Baba Jay, watching him tear open yet another packet of (my now nostalgic favorite— "World's Largest Selling") Parle-G biscuits to feed to another desperate mama-dog and her pups.

"It's better than starving," Baba Jay replied, as the mama-dog woofed down her treat, pups scrambling for her milk teats as they scamper off in a tumble.

So it's Baba Jay and his dogs I recall when the stewardess informs me she's got nothing to offer besides biscuits. I decide right then and there that white flour and white sugar will do me right in this case, and I break my rigid abstinence right then and there, to get some nourishment to my brain. I'm literally swallowing my pride, and I am immediately restored to sanity. The cookies are so good that I buy another packet.

Baba Jay is right. Being grateful for what's on offer IS better than starving.

Night Flight Fiasco
Kolkata Airport
November 21, 2007

The only thing worse than a fiasco involving a flight takeoff is not knowing what the source of the fiasco is.

A low-pitched male voice comes on the loudspeaker saying something slowly and deliberately in Bengali. I have no idea what is being said, except that everyone suddenly unbuckles their seatbelts, stands up, and begins taking the luggage down from the overhead compartments, queuing up to deplane, muttering unnervingly to themselves.

"What's happening?" I ask the nearest flight attendant.

"The flight is canceled," she replies.

"But why? Is something wrong with the plane? When will the flight to Goa leave, then?"

"No. It's Nandigram. The protests and riots have blocked the pilots from getting to the runway. We've missed our takeoff window for this flight to Goa. There is no other flight."

What the...? No other flight? I'd been following the news since I got to Kolkata, so I knew that the state of West Bengal was in serious political turmoil. Several people had been killed in the uprisings against the Communist seizure of agricultural lands in the rural district of Nandigram, seventy kilometers southwest of Kolkata. That year, farmers were getting serious about protecting their family property: the Communist (Marx-ist) government wanted to convert large sectors of agricultural land into "Special Economic Zones" (SEZs) for industrial development, ostensibly to diversify the West Bengal economy, which has always been a bread-basket of sorts for northeastern India. During the protests against land usury, many had died. Now, the aftermath of riots and outrage through-out the state capital had simply become known as "Nandigram."

It took a political revolution for my life to change forever.

The other stranded passengers and I step down from the plane, and the shuttle taxis us back to the terminal. Once we hit the airline informa-tion desk in a massive swarm of confusion, the Indians' outrage begins.

"What are we to do?"

"Something must be done!"

"We have traveled hours from our homes and villages to get here! *Where are we to go?*"

The pat answer is set to Repeat: "Sir (Madam), we are very sorry. But you can fly tomorrow."

It's nearing dusk. When I think of hitting the streets near the airport, which are literally on fire with strikes and riots, it doesn't make me feel any better. Something in my gut says I don't think I'm getting to Goa for my beach holiday.

Got to think quick! Think, Erin. Think! Across the shouting at the info booth, I've gleaned that I can't get a refund since I paid cash at the back-packer 'hood travel agency—that's a lost cause. I kick myself again for fly-ing—the seemingly luxurious travel mode, now made incredibly frustrat-ing. I want to try to speak with A Real Person With A Real Brain to find a possible solution, but there's no way I can compete with the throngs of Indians shouting, squeezing their way to the front of the queue, waving their boarding passes, fists in the air, demanding retribution.

I always marvel at Indians' behavior when a queue is involved. It's al-most as if the very idea of lining up in a straight fashion triggers a switch in the head, instructing, "Mayhem! Mayhem!"

Realizing that I'll be fighting the chaos for a good two hours before inching my way to the front of the madness, I haul ass back to the baggage claim carousel, catch sight of my pack, and throw it on my back— grateful I made the call to ship eight kilos back to the States just the day before—and trot as fast as I can toward the airport exit. Standing on the curb, I set down my pack, spark up a Gold Flake ciggie (traveler's vice— hey, it's an emergency pranayama), and take a few deep inhales to calm myself down.

I try to coast into a somewhat relaxed state of consciousness to see if I can catch a clue as to where to go now, what to do next. *Where in the hell can I transfer this ticket to now, in India, at the last minute, to arrive in the middle of the night?* My now ex-boyfriend, Tim, whom I've parted ways with because we grate on each other's nerves and my existential angst is out of control, is now long gone, two days prior. Tim is now in Tiruvannamalai, in Tamil Nadu, South India. I could try to catch up with him and fly to Chennai, but that flight isn't until tomorrow either. Night is falling, it's getting dark, and I… am… STUCK.

As I attempt to quiet my mind to see if a solution emerges, I suddenly recall an event that occurred just the previous evening in Kolkata.

I had visited a Catholic charity mission and shared chai with a lovely group of ladies—humble and devout Bengali Christian women. During our conversation, I had marveled at the faith of one strong widow in particular, as she recounted how she deals with big-time crises.

"When I don't know what to do in any given situation," she said confidently, "I PRAY." And at this—I swear—she actually *roared* with her whole heart. She continued, "And I say, God, YOU are my Heavenly Father. YOU got me into this situation. YOU will get me out. I DON'T HAVE ANYONE ELSE. So SHOW ME what YOUR will is. AMEN."

"And then," summing it up sweetly, setting her teacup down demurely yet with a graceful finality, she said, "I *trust*."

I am fervently remembering that sweet Bengali widow while I'm stranded on the curb in the Kolkata airport, and I follow suit right then and there. I stomp out the ciggie, close my eyes tightly, and proclaim to the Cosmos, "Okay, Universe. YOU got me into this situation. I have NO idea what to do, NOT ONE SINGLE CLUE. YOU get to get me out of this. I need a sign, God, NOW!"

I'm on autopilot now. I've dropped into witnessing mode. Since I have no idea what to do, *anything* that I do will simply have to do!

I walk to the information window at the passenger drop-off point near the curb. I presume I'll have a better chance of getting through to someone *outside*, since the rest of the pissed-off passengers are still mulling around *inside* the airport. I try to make eye contact with a clerk at the airline kiosk who appears to have an above-average intelligence gleam in her alert and pretty kohl-lined eyes.

She's got it: the look that says she is truly cognizant that I may actually need some real assistance.

"We cannot give you a refund, Madam. But we can fly you to Mumbai. That's the best I can do. It's the last flight anywhere tonight."

Mumbai. Mumbai. Oh my.

She means *Bombay*!

An urban agglomeration thrice the size of New York proper! Over eighteen million people on a jam-packed island of earth reclaimed from the sea. The fourth most populous city in the whole wide world—she wants me to fly there?! City of slum- and sidewalk-dwellers, Mafia, movies, and money (those who have lots and lots, and the absolutely have-nots)?

This, God, this Bombay is where you would have me go—arriving totally green, totally unprepared—in the MIDDLE of the flippin' NIGHT?

The computerized guidebook in my brain starts to whir to life. I'd avoided Bombay for years. It was the last big city in India for me to see, and I'd not seen any reason to subject myself. Until now, when I had no other choice.

What the hell would I want to go to Mumbai for?

I stand there, dumbfounded, mouth agape. As the seconds tick and the airline hostess waits impatiently for my answer, a sense of something greater than myself gradually envelops me. The pieces begin to click into place, and I'm clearly overcome with the eerie feeling that I am not in charge of any of this. It is as if something else is doing the leading.

Perhaps this *is* about being led. Prodded. Pulled. *Called.* For a very specific reason. And I think I know what that reason is.

"Transfer my ticket," I instruct the airline hostess. "I'll take the next plane out to Mumbai."

Interlude

In September 2007, before we had left San Francisco, Tim had keenly expressed interest in paying a visit to a well-respected sage by the name of Ramesh Balsekar when we got to India.

"He's considered a fully awakened master. Apparently, he's quite old but still giving talks in Bombay. Erin, *we gotta go see Ramesh!*"

Tim already had his own spiritual teacher—he wasn't looking for anything new himself; he was mostly encouraging the visit for *me* as he knew I had come to a plateau in my own journey. I earmarked the name—*Ramesh*—and put it far in the back burners of my mind. It sounded intriguing enough: a wise, little old Indian man in some small flat somewhere in scarily huge Bombay, dispensing wisdom to a few lucky seekers who tracked down his personal address.

But while Tim and I were on our India expedition together, traversing most of the important Hindu and Buddhist pilgrimage hotspots in North India while disagreeing and arguing half the time, I'd had more "spiritual" on my plate than I ever could eat. Culminating in the "call off the search" experience at Papaji's home in Lucknow, I'd come to realize there was Nothing to search for.

I was, quite simply, *done.*

Just plain done with the whole damn thing. Frankly, I didn't care if I ever reached enlightenment, whatever the hell that was anyway.

It didn't seem to matter what I did or didn't do to improve myself or become more peaceful. No matter how hard I tried, no matter how much I meditated, how long I was abstinent from this person or that thing or this or that thought, my romantic relationships still ended in disaster after disaster, and depression and emotional upheaval still paid me regular visits.

I'd read bushels of spiritual and self-improvement books, sat hundreds of hours in silence, practiced the arts of astrology, celibacy, and even staying sugar-free.

I'd visited oodles of ashrams, teachers, and holy spots over the course of three major odysseys to India and a lifetime of spiritual questing, and I was still the same Erin. Yes, albeit a strong Erin, and a smart Erin, and a good-person Erin. But there didn't seem to be an appropriate, end-of-the-line, keep it simple and keep it REAL *teacher* anywhere in the world for me. I was still miserable.

Sometimes, I simply hated my life, even if it was good and even if it seemed charmed to others. The worst part was that, due to my existential angst, I simply could not get along with any boyfriend, though I deeply craved companionship, affection, and partnership.

I had come to the end of my rope.

I was so miserable, I could do nothing *but* accept that This, apparently, *is* as Good as It Gets.

I was veritably done with All Things Spiritual and even more done with anything resembling a guru, teacher, truth, way, or "path."

Still, being ever the curious cat, I had told Tim that if we happened to pass through Mumbai toward the tail end of our journey, well then, I'd have a gander, go visit Ramesh, and receive some darshan.

I'd completely forgotten about the whole thing, until one day in October. Tim and I were staying in Rishikesh. One morning, I was having coffee alone in a little café overlooking the Ganges. I happened to sit next to a Dutchman named David, whom I had met the year prior on an overnight train from Delhi. David and I said our hellos and remembrances and talked about what it was like to be back in India again one year later. He explained he was primarily in India to get to Bombay and spend as much time as possible with his teacher.

"Who is it?" I inquired, skeptical and fed up with the whole holy matter.

"His name is Ramesh," replied David, showing me the cover of the book he was reading. "He's a teacher of the principles found in *I Am That*. I'm sure you've heard of it, the famous book on Advaita, *Talks with Sri Nisargadatta Maharaj*?"

I had indeed heard of *I Am That*. In fact, I'd come across this powerful book on philosophy the very first time I'd come to Rishikesh, in 2002. The big, dense, black-and-yellow book was too much for me when I'd first peeked inside, far too "beyond the beyond." It was a language I could not grasp at the time, with themes like the world being an illusion—*maya*—and that we are only a reflection of the Source, not the reality; we are only a reflection of reality appearing as if a dream.

That was a bit too way-out, even for me, back then. I couldn't conceive how everything was merely a reflection of the Ultimate, how this waking life was as much of a dream as the dreamtime. *And how would that help me live my daily life, anyway?*

Later that evening, I mentioned my brief encounter with David the Dutchman to Tim. "He was talking about that Ramesh Balsekar guy in Mumbai," I said.

"See, Erin! We need to go see him!" Tim replied.

But my interest in this teacher, Ramesh, wasn't duly ignited until, two days later walking past the same coffee shop, I caught a glimpse of David again out of the corner of my eye. Before I'd even fully registered that it was him, I got an instantaneous, split-second but unmistakably strong shock in the center of my chest. Imagine the shock from those electric paddles used to bring back a person having a heart attack, or the spark of jumper cables used to restart a car battery.

What the hell... was that? I never mentioned it to anyone, neither

Tim nor David, at the time. I only knew it was some weird phenomenon around the heart, like a quick-start, and it was something I'd never experienced before. It was kind of scary, in a good way.

Was THAT some sort of weird SIGN or something about this teacher Ramesh, that thing *that people talk about?* I wondered.

Even though I was sure the experience was totally impersonal, that I had no interest in David, I wasn't about to tell my boyfriend Tim that I had just gotten some random electric heart-shock-thing from another man.

I filed the incident away until that day of destiny, when I was stuck, stranded and alone, at the Kolkata International Airport in the middle of the night.

With an invalid ticket. With nowhere to go, nothing I could do.

And there was only one place to which they would fly: Mumbai.

I was terrified of the unknown, but sure there was a greater plan at hand, a plan that had both nothing and everything to do with me.

I was standing on that airport curb, trying to decide whether to take the airline's offer, and I suddenly remembered that shock to the heart. At that point in time, meeting Ramesh was the only reason I would have ever stepped foot in the largest city in India in the middle of the night. *That whole "shock thing," and now this crazy canceled flight—is this sort of thing what they mean when they talk about the "call of the guru"?*

But I had given up the search for a teacher, for a path! I had made the decision that I was going to live my life as it was, and just see how it all played out. If there was pain, I'd endure it. If there was pleasure, I'd enjoy it. There was nothing more I could do, because there was nothing to find… and I'd simply exhausted myself trying.

And that's when it happened.

PART II
The Teacher Appears

Waking Up in Mumbai
Mumbai (Bombay)
November 22, 2007

I arrived just after midnight in that terrifying, nocturnal Mumbai megalopolis.

With no choice, I *had* to trust, every single scared-shitless second of the way. Unfamiliar with this city and unaware of the airport's pre-paid taxi stand, I was ripped off straight out of the gate by a cabbie with a rigged meter. At least I made it to the hotel safely, luggage and person in one piece. It was the cheapest hotel in rapid rupee-sucking Bombay I could find, The Hotel Gemini, located (I'd come to find out later) in dodgy Khetwadi and lanes of questionable activity.

With strange men and strange Hindi conversations going on a foot next to me through paper-thin walls, I kept reminding myself there was nothing to fear, that everything would be okay, as it always is. The hotel boy ordered me in a late-night plate of chapati and aloo gobi. Gratefully, I devoured the food, washed up, and went to sleep, wondering where the hell I'd landed and how I'd get by in this massive city.

I woke up at the crack of dawn the next morning. It was Thanksgiving Day. I was physically exhausted, but another part of me seemed completely awake and aware of every move in this bizarre movie appearing in my life's theater, this *lila*. I readied myself to meet Ramesh, his address jotted down from a lucky two minutes nabbed in the Kolkata airport Internet café just before takeoff.

I concentrated on staying calm as I got dressed and sipped a strong cup of Nescafe. Just before leaving the hotel to hail a cab, I wrote in my journal:

> *I have no idea why I am here.*
> *I was pulled here by a power beyond me.*
> *I am going with absolutely no expectations.*
> *I have nothing to lose.*
> *Let's see what happens…*

Ramesh and his family occupied the top floor of a handsome residential building on a peaceful, leafy street in a classy seaside Mumbai neighborhood called Breach Candy. I arrived at Ramesh's home just before 9 a.m.—the start time of daily satsang. The kind doorman told me to go to the fourth floor, motioning to the old-fashioned elevator in the building lobby. I took the gated lift, noting the carriage played a merry, slightly distorted and tinkly tune as it rose to the top floor. The elevator stopped, and upon exiting, I noticed a heap of shoes piled up outside a door to my right. Following the lead, I slipped off my sandals, then pushed open the door, which was slightly ajar.

Immediately, I was welcomed by a kind-faced man introducing himself as Murthy. I noticed about a dozen other folks—a mix of Indians and Westerners—seated in the large living room just off the entryway. This spacious main room was tastefully decorated with a blend of traditional Indian and modern artwork and attractively furnished with a pleasant, welcoming feel. Several large, partly open windows allowed fresh air, beautiful blue skies, and morning light to flow into the room.

Still standing in the entryway, Murthy asked if I had been there before. Nervously, I answered no. He then asked if I had any questions for Ramesh.

"Quite honestly, I have no idea," I replied. "But since I came all this way, I may as well speak to him!"

Murthy escorted me to sit in what I would later find out was called "the hot seat," a chair placed directly before a cushioned rocking chair at the front of the room. I took a deep breath and tried to settle in. A few seconds passed, and I heard the shuffling of feet behind me. Turning to see what was coming, I spotted a slight, elderly Indian man walking swiftly to the front of the room.

Ramesh.

Wearing a simple outfit of white trousers and white shirt, barefoot, downy crown of white hair, no teeth—Ramesh beamed clear energy. His tiny form couldn't hold a candle to the energy exuded. Ramesh sat down in the rocking chair before me and immediately greeted me with a pleasant hello.

"Hello," I responded, then dropped into my inner self and took a deep breath as Ramesh jumped into conversation with me, giving me no time to think. *Open heart, speak from the heart,* I reminded myself. Our conversation began with Ramesh asking me a series of questions.

"What is your name?"

"My name is Erin."

"And which part of the world do you come from?"

"The U.S."

"And how do you make your living?"

"I am a writer."

"Writer. What sort of things do you write about?"

"Stories. About India. And spiritual experience."

"I see, I see. And what brings you here today?"

"I have a friend, who is a student of Advaita and Ramana Maharshi, who told me about you. And I've read some things from your teacher, Sri Nisargadatta Maharaj."

"I see. And what made you interested in all this?"

"Spiritual experiences, I suppose."

"And how long have you been having these experiences?"

"My whole life. Ever since I can remember."

"And what is the nature of these experiences?"

"Probably the simplest way I can answer that is to say that, in my direct experience, when I surrender and leave it all to God, I find that miracles do happen and I am also much, much more peaceful."

"And you have learned about the spiritual from where?"

"Since birth. And, of course, reading."

"What books have you read? Where did you go? With whom did you speak?"

I am all at once totally and completely stunned. Suddenly aware of a video camera directly focused on me, my mind has gone completely blank. I cannot think of a single spiritual book I've read at this moment save The Celestine Prophecy, *which I read in 1992 and which I consider a New Age teeth-cutter.*

I'm honestly at a loss for words, but I muddle on to answer Ramesh's question.

"I'm completely disarmed. I wasn't expecting this in the least. I never expected to find myself here. The books aren't so important."

"So you aren't much of a reader. More of a writer."

"Yes."

"So you have been a seeker your whole life? And what is it that you are seeking?"

I take a deep breath. I have come so far and have been dropped from the sky to be here at this moment. I want to be totally honest, but hope to God it doesn't come out of my mouth sounding foolish.

"Peace. And freedom."

That is my honest answer, straight from the heart.

"Freedom from what?"

"Freedom from suffering. Or the illusion of suffering."

"I see. Well, let me tell you about who I am and what I talk about..."

Ramesh then proceeded to explain to me, with crystal clarity, how everything was a happening in Consciousness.

"Events happen, deeds are done, but there is no individual or experiencer thereof," he said. This made perfect sense, confirming what I always knew 100 percent, deep in my heart: *I am not in charge.*

"Thy will be done," confirmed Ramesh. My heart sang with glee when I heard Ramesh say these words—words I was all too familiar with but needed confirmed with absolute certainty. I was not responsible for this suffering! I didn't cause it, and I am not doing anything wrong, because I have no control over the outcome. I'm not causing this pain, and I'm not causing these ongoing relationship dramas. It's all part of the cosmic play, the *lila!*

"There is no individual doer," explained Ramesh. I understood: there was nothing *I* could do about my horrific existential suffering. The emotional pain and mental anguish would last as long as it would last, until it ends. The seeking itself *is* the suffering! Consciousness started the seeking, and Consciousness (God's will, Cosmic Law) would end it.

My soul exhaled deeply, my mind relaxed completely. This was a complete and total relief, an end of the load of guilt and shame, an end of the insidiousness of pride and egoic identification, an end of seeking for something to *do* to fix my life! "Life is impersonal functioning of Totality. There is no one doing anything. Everything just happens," taught Ramesh.

Hallelujah!

I spent three days and three nights in Mumbai, attending morning satsangs at Ramesh's residence. I was awestruck, focused, and completely taken by the non-dual teachings. From the very first presentation of Truth that Ramesh presented, it confirmed everything I'd always known, but never had a completely clear mirror to reflect it back to me.

I was higher than a kite and accepted Ramesh as my *guru du jour* hook, line, and sinker, on the spot. I could not say he was my GURU, with a capital G. Oh, no… that was too much. I wasn't at all sure about the whole guru-and-devotion thing, and thus it was easier to joke and say that I had a teacher for the moment, my guru du jour.

Intellectually, I grokked the entire conversation with Ramesh that first day in the hot seat. I received on-the-spot *jnana,* or intellectual understanding, though I knew there had to be an embodiment of faith too, one that occurs deep in the Heart, known as *bhakti*.

I couldn't afford to stay longer than a few days in Mumbai. It was both too expensive for my meager backpacker budget, and it was also a taxing place to stay emotionally and physically—super stimulating. Plus, I'd received all the insight and transmission I could handle in that first three days. I needed to integrate!

Attempting to continue on to southern India, to a paradisiacal village that I'd stayed in many times before located along the Konkan Coast of Karnataka, I made an inadvertent side trip. For no reason at all, I got on the wrong connecting train, and instead of heading south to Karnataka, I ended up in the middle of nowhere in the jungles of eastern Goa; no services, nothing around. Catching the last train back to the transport hub, night was falling and it was too late to catch a bus or train further south, so I stayed in a resort beach area in southern Goa for two nights. During the day, I sat in an outdoor café totally blissed out. Every song on the café radio was like a love song from God, to God.

Two days later, I headed further south to the Konkan Coast to spend time at the beach during Christmas. During this time, I read one chapter each morning of Ramesh's book, *Peace and Harmony in Daily Living*. Every sentence rang true in my heart and mind.

I couldn't write a word in my journal at the time. Those first mind-blowing epiphanies and awakenings were too intense. It was all settling in, integrating. I was so excited to finally have a Teacher—at last.

Truth be told, I never expected to have a guru in this life. I could never imagine I'd meet a spiritual force in a physical body that I would trust 100 percent, with all my heart and soul, to lay down my suffering.

Caught in the Tiger's Jaw

For the next three years, I remained primarily in India, with two short visits back to the U.S. to address family and business matters. I divided my time between sitting in satsang with Ramesh in Mumbai, living in South India along the seaside of Karnataka, and journeying further afield to explore India in all Her glory—north, east, south, and west. While on the road, I continued to pen travel tales, both for freelance travel magazine gigs as well as my Bindi Girl *stories.*

The following chapters convey my experience of integrating, deepening, and realizing non-dual (Advaita) wisdom as spiritual knowledge (jnana). Like the finger pointing to the moon is not the moon, these essays point to the full impact of these teachings as direct transmission from a realized master. The fierce grace received from Ramesh fully permeated my heart and exploded in my being as bhakti—*divine love and devotion, at which point I could easily say that Ramesh was, indeed, my Guru.*

Those on whom the Guru's glance
Of grace has fallen are like the deer
Caught in a tiger's jaw. They are bound
To have their wretched ego slain
And know the one supreme Awareness.
They will never be forsaken.
~ *Sri Ramana Maharshi*

Through the Net
Konkan Coast
November 5, 2008

Six years after boarding that first night flight to India in 2002, I write this from my retreat in South India. I am still a gypsy—I don't have a permanent home, and I still live out of my backpack. I have two "bases" in India—one on the beach here along the Konkan Coast in Karnataka and one in Bombay. The latter, I visit every six to eight weeks in order to see Ramesh.

For now, I am home.

In eternal gratitude.

OM shanti OM.

Following is a beautiful passage from Sri Nisargadatta Maharaj, who was Ramesh's Advaita guru. Interestingly, these lines were first sent to me in May 2007 by a mentor-friend, Jim Fadiman, who wanted to give me a small gift of thanks for my ongoing travel writing blog. At the time, I'd never heard of Sri Nisargadatta, nor Advaita, though I loved the quote.

The real world is beyond the mind's ken;
we see it through the net of our desires,
divided into pleasure and pain,
right and wrong, inner and outer.
To see the universe as it is, you must step beyond the net.
It is not hard to do so, for the net is full of holes.
~ Sri Nisargadatta Maharaj, *I Am That*

Who Are You?
Konkan Coast
December 5, 2008

Who are you?
Who who, who who
I really wanna know...
~ Pete Townshend of The Who

All I knew was: "I must leave today, *today*, TODAY for Mumbai!"
Time to put aside the uncertainty. The concern and doubt.
Pray for protection and peace.
And go.
Ever since the November 26, 2008 terrorist attacks on Mumbai, known
as "26/11," I had been trying to get back in touch with pure, positive ener-
gy. With so much fear and negativity flying around the west coast of India,
the only thing I could do was stay connected to my heart, to the Source.

After a good, solid week of spiritual solace, being in Nature, a lot of
rest and eating right, it was time to leave the beaches of South India and
return to beloved Bombay. I wanted to pay my respects to a city that had
irrefutably changed my life. I also needed to take care of a few items of
business, and—most importantly—see my teacher.

I had been notified that my aging guruji had fallen ill; at ninety-one,
it appeared he may soon enter mahasamadhi. I recalled hearing a story

about the kirtan musician, Krishna Das, who had a vision that he should get back to India to see his guru, Neem Karoli Baba ("Maharaji"). Krishna Das was a bit caught up back in the world, in New York, and thus did not heed the call. Maharaji passed away before Krishna Das got to say goodbye face to face.

Needless to say, I had to get my butt back to Bombay.

I didn't care that I'd have to take an eighteen-hour train, without reservations, without a sleeper bunk. The heart gives a strength from beyond.

At the local railway station, traveling with, as per usual, too much stuff, I hauled myself and my luggage up to the platform. After I dropped my bags on the concrete floor, I overheard a young French backpacker, wearing a très stylish red-and-black fedora, discussing his upcoming overnight bus journey from Goa to Mumbai, as he could not get a train booked to Mumbai.

"Heading home?" I asked, assuming that anyone taking that hellish overnight bus is desperate to catch a flight.

"Yes, unfortunately!" he replied.

"That's okay, you'll be back!" I said.

"*Mais oui!*" the Frenchman agreed. "*Absolutement.*"

Besides the French backpacker, I'd also noticed a bright and shiny young man perched on the platform between us and all my bags. It wasn't until the golden-haired stranger turned and addressed me directly that I noticed he was a doppelganger of my former travel partner, Tim. With the exception of his subtle lip piercing and lovely London accent, I felt I could have been speaking to my old friend.

Now, this tall and muscular, blond-haired and blue-eyed Brit—*Chris*, as he introduced himself—turned to strike up a conversation. We chit-chatted for a bit: how long I'd been in India, where I'd been, favorite places—the usual. Chris was particularly interested in hearing what it took for me to make the transition to living in India, and about material renouncement, the uncertainties of the future, and the guts it takes to follow your bliss.

Gorgeous, twenty-something Chris said he had been a professional dancer in London, working on music videos and stage shows before blowing out his knee last year. Absolutely clueless as to what he should do next, and perhaps influenced by his Bikram Yoga teacher, he decided to come to India.

"I guess I was looking for some sort of epiphany here," Chris said. He was searching for The Answer to that all-pervading question hanging over the heads of so many young (and old) Westerners everywhere: *What should I do with my life?*

"Since this injury to my knee happened, and I can't dance professionally anymore, I gotta figure out what to do," explained Chris. "I've traveled all over India the past three months," he said, "and I still haven't got my epiphany. And I've only got four days left!"

Despite my usual standard of keeping my opinion to myself (unless solicited), I couldn't help myself in this case. A reaction flew out of my mouth:

"With all due respect," I began, "I have to say, I believe the reason you haven't gotten your answer is that it's the wrong question..." My words drifted off, as I wasn't really expecting Chris to be up for hearing philosophical dribble.

"Really? Tell me more." Chris leaned toward me on our shared bench, surprising me with his keen interest.

"Well," I continued, "I just hear so many folks running in circles, chasing their tails, asking themselves what they should do with themselves. Honestly, have you ever known anyone to actually get an *answer* to that question?"

"Actually, no!" he answered. "That's true!"

"That's because the very question is non-resourceful." I went on, since he seemed interested, and our train was late anyway. "The very question, 'what should I do?' doesn't work, and only invites frustration and anxiety. It can't be answered. In my opinion, and, more importantly, in my direct experience, we are not human *doings*. We are human *beings*. If we identify ourselves with what we *do*, it is a setup for disappointment."

"Go on," encouraged Chris.

Since he seemed to know I wasn't proselytizing, I continued. "I have found that the better question is 'Who Am I?' Find out who you *are*. The true you, I believe, is pure Source, or Consciousness. That is the truth that is never changing. If we can get in touch with *that*, my experience is that the 'doing' takes care of itself. Life, or Nature, is the real director, and we humans naturally do whatever Life has designed us to do as a natural expression of who we are. We don't even have to think one iota about it."

"That totally makes sense!" Chris was really getting into it now; I could see it in his eyes. "It's… it's… *organic*."

"Exactly! That's the *exact* word for it." I couldn't believe these words were coming from my lips. I was talking in hushed tones so as not to attract attention from the other backpackers sitting nearby. Although I didn't care if they heard, I wasn't into sounding like a preacher. It was simply a conversation…

A conversation that simply *happened*. Naturally. Spontaneously. Organically.

Now, Chris put two and two together and made it clearer for both of us. "Ah, I see, so if we identify ourselves with what we *do*, and the thing we're doing doesn't work out, then we feel like it's *us* that has failed."

"Yes," I affirmed.

"And if we focus on who we *are*, we can't go wrong!"

"Yes."

"Wow." Chris looked directly and soulfully into my eyes. "I think I just got that epiphany."

A whistle blew. Our train was arriving on the platform. As we gathered our bags, I happened to glimpse golden rays of light streaming between Chris and me. At that moment, that fleeting phenomenon of bliss, I realized that Chris was the real bearer of gifts.

In that five-minute chat on the railway platform, this stranger had embodied the truth, the whole truth and nothing but the truth. Like a big, gorgeous mirror, smiling and waving right back, declaring loud and clear—just like that whistle-blowing train barreling into the station:

"Helloooooooo, Erin! You *are* on the right track."

And with that great boost of confidence and grace, I boarded the train bound for Mumbai, knowing beyond the shadow of a doubt, whatever happened, I would be fine.

Just fine.

No matter what.

> *The very act of perceiving shows you are not what you perceive.*
> *You are the limitless being.*
> ~ Sri Nisargadatta Maharaj, *I Am That*

Some Like It Hot
Mumbai
Pre-Monsoon 2009

Cooking, frying, sizzling in Mumbai's pre-monsoon heat, I arose pre-dawn, hoping for a moment of coolness, and checked the temperature. It was a hundred and eight *inside* my hotel room.

Unbelievable, I laughed to myself. *Just call me Sweaty Betty.*

I was hell-bent and determined to sweat it out in the sweltering city, to partake in the final series of satsang talks given by my Advaita Teacher before he was certain to make a permanent physical departure at the age of ninety-two. These were Ramesh's last days… Nothing could pry me away. I was on fire—Kundalini fire from the moment I landed.

In early May, I'd left India to go back to the U.S., planning for a reprieve from India's hottest months; but my heart could not stay away—the power of love was too strong. I had to get back, so just two weeks later, I hopped on a plane for the twenty-plus hour return flight to Mumbai. I made it back just in time to Ramesh's *jayanti* (birthday) celebration the morning of May 25, and from that day on, I was cooking…

My computer got zapped with a weird virus the day I arrived—total hard drive meltdown. Clearly, I wasn't supposed to work.

Mumbai boasts the most expensive accommodation prices in India—I couldn't afford a monthly room with air-con. Mornings I would go to satsang, and afternoons I would lie in my non-AC cracker box with the fan whirling the hot, ninety-nine percent humidity stuffy air over my sweaty body, and cry.

The Kundalini energy rising up through the spinal column *nadi* channels, triggered partially by the heat and partially by the intensity of the spiritual transmission I was receiving, was actually painful, disturbing at best. I was completely—physically and electrically—maxed out. Zaps and zings, shorts and starts electrified my heart center. I thought I might be electrocuting myself.

Not to mention, I thought I'd go mad with sexual energy, the vibration with which I could equate the fiery current buzzing up the chakras. One night I was so *hot*, I stood outside the door of a fellow disciple—a good-looking German who lived down the hall at my guest house—hand raised and ready to knock. As I stood there in my sweaty nightgown, I had to talk myself down from a blatant, late-night booty call.

"Back to bed with you, young lady," I told myself, and marched back to my own room and into a cold shower.

Dragging my overly hot ass through daily life, I was determined to stay in Bombay one full month, a twenty-eight-day lunar cycle. I knew that opportunities like this—timing, resources, aged Teacher actually giving talks still—don't come calling all the time. So, I endured four showers a day to try to cool off.

I'd lie awake at 4 a.m., waiting for dawn, clutching my pen and dripping sweat on the pages of my journal. When the first rays of light sprung over the Victorian clock tower outside my window, I'd don shorts and walking sandals and head to the Churchgate cricket *maidan* for a lightning-fast sun salutation session or a brisk speed-walk around the track. Always tricky: finish your workout before the voyeurs find you. I knew I was pushing it wearing shorts—my knees were showing. I only had a tiny window of opportunity, immediately after sunrise, before I was discovered as the early-morning white girl attraction.

The month of June was even more unbearable, as the monsoon rains were now three weeks late, and the pressure buildup resembled a hot water balloon in a vise, compressed to the breaking point.

For me, however, the inner heat was more than a pre-monsoon blasting barometer or throbbing thermometer. It was the energetic and emotional transformation I was undergoing as a result of attending daily satsangs and the proximity with my spiritual teacher. I would sit in satsang and feel a sort of electric *buzzzzzzz* running through my being. It was like sitting in some sort of MRI tunnel or full-body Reiki chamber. I figured it was what the traditional spiritual teachings are referring to when they discuss transmission from a Master. I realized that my Teacher was probably exuding something beyond the beyond—all the prana, all the wisdom—for the students to absorb during these final days as his tiny physical form was evaporating before our eyes. These last days, Ramesh seemed to be operating almost exclusively from a pranic, etheric body.

One morning, I couldn't stop crying—sobbing, rather. At my guest house, feeling completely wretched, I donned oversized Jackie O sunglasses then clambered into a cab, dragging myself uptown to my Teacher's house. My beloved guru was perched in his favorite chair in his private room with his beautiful wife, Sharda, by his side. I removed the dark glasses and greeted the two radiant beings in namaskar fashion, bowing my head, kneeling, and touching my head to His feet in traditional Indian guru-disciple manner.

"Guruji," I pleaded, kneeling before him, "this is all much too intense!"

"I know your understanding has gone very, very deep," Ramesh replied in the sweet way he spoke, toothless and using the last bit of his vital essence to speak only the most necessary words. His physique was so frail; his gray-blue-brown eyes, however, were blazing like infernos of pure light.

Damn straight, I thought. *The understanding has gone so deep, it's literally rewiring my entire internal electrical structure!* I hoped my Teacher might turn the volume down a bit, or somehow put me out of my psychospiritual-physical misery.

"Have you written yet about the teaching?" Ramesh asked me gently and kindly.

"Not yet," I replied. "I'm going crazy! I know that none of this matters, and I really do not care AT ALL about anything anymore—that it's all maya," I blubbered, chest heaving, still sobbing. "I just want it all to finish, go all the way. I feel completely crazy—mad!"

I felt like I needed some sort of release valve for all the energy, like the Kundalini energy could pierce and spout out of the top of my head like a big sparkly fountain or something.

"You know we can't want anything!" Ramesh said lovingly to me, with a twinkle in his eyes and a slight smile.

He'd dinged me on the flaw in my understanding. I knew what he said to be totally true, that there wasn't a damned thing I could do, so I just closed my eyes and meditated, seated on the floor before His Lotus Feet. After just a few seconds, I felt a wave of cooling energy slowly come over me and a pulling down into the earth of all the excess crown chakra energy that had built up. It helped; by Grace, the volume turned down a bit, so that I could endure the activity of Kundalini shakti without being fried to total madness.

Later that day, an Australian disciple friend, Rani, fed me homemade soup, chapati, and ice water in her air-conditioned apartment. She then directed me to a bathtub filled with water and ice cubes, where I sat and cried for an hour while constantly pouring cold water over my head. After a sesame oil self-massage, a nap, and Shiatsu session from Rani, the color had returned to my cheeks.

Things improved tremendously, though it was still up and down with the Kundalini activity and the barometer levels. One day the pressure was so intense, it literally cut glass:

I'd met a hot (in the handsome sense) Romanian Gemini at satsang. He was my age, smart, charming, and spiritual—just my type. Stefan and I were fast becoming friends, and I was boiling inside, on more levels than one. One morning after the talks, we met for chai at the neighborhood café.

Stefan was open-minded, and we could talk about anything, really. I was explaining the burning I'd been experiencing, coupled with the intense fiery sensations and sexual tension pulsing through my body. Perhaps to lighten up the conversation, Stefan replied with a slightly mocking comment, with the teeniest hint of jest. I felt a bit hurt—maybe because he didn't get the hint that, clearly, I needed an outlet. I thought I might burst.

At that moment, the smirking Stefan picked up his freshly filled water glass that stood between us. Upon being lifted, the glass cleanly sliced itself in half before our eyes, the entire base falling to the tabletop. Cold water gushed out all over the table, splashing everywhere and soaking the two of us in the process. Stefan's jaw dropped.

"I told you. It's intense," I said.

Ultimately, I had to catch a train to South India, to recuperate seaside and solo, where the rains had already arrived, to cool off and quench my raging fire.

Got Stars in His Eyes
Mumbai
August 8, 2009

My beloved Guruji is in the hospital ICU, preparing for hip surgery. I visited him today, and he looked so beautiful lying there, resting quietly. His color was good—browner and healthier than the last time I saw him—and he was sleeping peacefully.

I felt so nervous entering his most personal of spaces—the Intensive Care Unit. The primary reason for my visit to Mumbai was to pay my last respects. To express my love and gratitude, and if I were lucky—if it were my destiny—I'd have five minutes to sit in The Teacher's presence and receive his *darshan*. I'd snuck into the ward five minutes before official visiting hours began; no one else was around.

I entered the hospital room slowly. I could see he was asleep. Ramesh's darshan was so powerful. The field emanated from his small body, thin but strong, lying on the elevated hospital bed.

I looked around. I was pleased and impressed with the cleanliness, tidiness, and organization of the Breach Candy hospital room. I settled in at a chair by his bedside.

Guruji awoke and opened his eyes.

"Hello there," he said quietly as he looked over at me. I immediately stood and rushed to his side. I told him I had come up to Bombay from

South India to tell him that I loved him and that he looked beautiful.

He said, "That wasn't necessary." I noticed that his tousled hair looked like white duckling down. And then he really opened his eyes wide, and we looked at each other for several moments.

THE STARS IN HIS EYES WERE SO BRIGHT.

I could barely look into them. They were beautiful and fascinating—a gray-blue twinkling and sheer solar radiance emanating. They were two suns blazing.

I sat down when he closed his eyes again, but a force pulled me up out of my chair and to his bedside. "Guruji! You have *stars* in your eyes!"

"What?" he asked, waking up all over again.

"Your eyes—they're so bright, they're like stars!"

"Thank you," he replied, and gazed at me a bit longer. He blinked a few times while looking at me. *Bling bling bling*—his eyes sparked in my direction.

Sitting back down to take it in, I immediately thought of a line:

"My guru's eyes are the stars."

Never knowing if it was going to be the last time, I kissed him good-bye on the cheek.

PART III
The Teacher Disappears

Experience of Immortality

The last time I saw my guru, Ramesh Balsekar, in person was August 2009. Right after I visited him in the hospital, I intuited a message from my guru that would help deepen my understanding. The message I received that August afternoon was about the final dropping of ego identification. In this reverie, Ramesh spoke to me—a disciple who had been experiencing the flip-flop between total non-involvement (nobody home, no separate "me") and occasional involvement with the ego identification—as follows:

Erin, it's basically about timepassing. Total realization is inevitable if there is full intellectual understanding, so keep working on intellectual understanding in the meantime. Read my reflections on Jnaneshwar's Experience of Immortality. *You might enjoy Jnaneshwar because he is also a* bhakta-jnani *like you.*

I picked up *Experience of Immortality* at my favorite Indian philosophy and spirituality bookstore, Chetana, in the Fort neighborhood. Knowing that there was nothing I could do in Mumbai except wait indefinitely for Ramesh to either come back to health or leave the body, I took the train back to my village in the South Indian state of Karnataka.

Reading the book over the next month, at the tail end of the monsoon rains, the great sage Jnaneshwar completely blew my mind—or what was left of it. Every day was like an orgasmic explosion of understanding and realization. And it's not an easy read! I've heard *Experience of Immortality* described as Ramesh's most challenging yet most rewarding work.

Like the Tao, the text is paradoxical and cannot be grasped with the linear mind. For me, reading with diffuse awareness, in the right frame of mind, is most effective. I find reading sacred texts extremely early in the morning (between the hours of 3:30 a.m. and sunrise) is best for absorbing wisdom.

On September 27, 2009, I was reading the final chapter of the book during my usual morning reading, reflecting, and note-taking time. I "got it" upside down and every way. That very morning, I finished the book with tremendous gratitude thumping through my being.

After my morning yoga practice, I sat in meditation on my deck for a long time—longer than usual. Upon opening my eyes, I saw a radiant white and sparkly aura emanating from my body and all around me— *God is in the house.* I was brought to tears as I felt Ramesh's presence, and the power of truth and love, so deeply.

At lunchtime, I sat in my favorite locale enjoying a thali of rice and dal, basking in the glory of simple Existence. Just then, I received a text message from Rachel, a fellow American disciple of Ramesh's who was up in Mumbai.

"Erin, how are you? Do you know?"

I almost dropped the phone. That was the moment of the deafening roar of silence. I didn't even need to call or text my friend. I knew.

Ramesh was gone. He had taken mahasamadhi at 9 a.m., exactly as I was practicing yoga on the deck, basking in the white light of pure Love— the very morning I finished the treatise, *The Experience of Immortality.*

HARI OM TAT SAT

Ramesh Balsekar

May 25, 1917—September 27, 2009

Beloved Ramesh

Konkan Coast
September 27, 2009

There are no words
I am only in my heart
Silence. Love. Gratitude.
Letting images and music speak for me...
OOOOOOooooooommmmmmmmmMMMMM
Beloved Guruji
Ramesh Balsekar
May 25, 1917 - September 27, 2009
On the Ninth Day of Navaratri,
the Nine Nights of the Goddess
At Nine o'clock in the morning
In the Ninth Month of September,
the year two thousand and Nine
on the 27th (2+7=9)
the Ninth Night of Navaratri,
the Nine Nights of the Goddess
on the final day,
the power of Durga Puja,
in which we celebrate Smasana Kali,

Goddess of the Cremation Grounds…
Beloved Guruji
Ramesh Balsekar
has merged
with
the Great Ocean
of Consciousness
There are no words.
Only Love.
Bhakti. Bhajan.
For You.
Love.
sat * chit * ananda
being * consciousness * peace

*It does not matter whether you get Enlightened or not before you die.
After death the identified consciousness of a psychopath
and that of a Sage merge with the same Source.
It makes no difference to the Ocean
whether the dirtiest water or the purest Ganga merges with it.*
~ Ramesh Balsekar

Death Rattle

On September 27, 2009, at 9 a.m. on the ninth day of the Navratri festival of the Goddess, my beloved teacher, guru, and spiritual friend Ramesh Balsekar took mahasamadhi at his home in Bombay. Mahasamadhi is when a realized master finally and intentionally leaves the body to merge with the infinite. Since there is no ego identification, it is said that a sage enters the ultimate (maha) non-dual consciousness (samadhi).

When I got the call, I was an overnight train ride away and knew I couldn't get north in time for the cremation pyre. That day, my world stopped. There was only silence, and that silence was deafening. Never again would I behold the great spirit and force of Nature that was my guru as embodied Consciousness, in the flesh, known as Ramesh.

I was only beginning to understand the indescribable union between teacher and student that occurs in a guru-disciple relationship; there is a fusion of hearts and minds that makes it possible for the soul to surrender identification with the ego. It seems to be a combination of the power of defeat and the power of love.

In the days and months that followed my Teacher's passing, my soul experienced an overpowering transformation: intense grief at the loss of a part of my self, somewhat like an amputation, combined with a quickening. It was as if this body-mind known as Erin had been placed into a sort of quantum microwave. In a microwave, all the particles are scat-

tered about, vibrating faster than the speed of light, disembodied from the original matter even though things still appear cohesive. Amazingly, such a vibrating mass of consciousness appears to be a whole substance, but there is really only empty space between particles, and empty space within those same particles. Finally, there is only empty space.

And my own "empty space" was getting cooked. My soul wanted to leave the body and dissolve into Consciousness to join Ramesh. Over the next two months, I couldn't ground. My sister Nerine came to visit me from Berlin—her first visit to India—a trip that had been planned for months, scheduled to begin just a week after Ramesh's unforeseen passing. I was both lucky and grateful to have my sister with me and simultaneously irritated and half sick; the grief was horrific, and I had no interest in playing tour guide up in North India.

Moving too fast while preparing to leave the south, I fell down a flight of stairs in a monsoon downpour and could have broken my neck. I stopped in Mumbai en route north so that I could attend a memorial service for Ramesh; the heartbreak was excruciating. In Rishikesh, I slipped and smashed my tailbone on a moss-covered bathing platform while stepping into the Ganges to offer flowers during puja. Twice (once in Varanasi and once in Rishikesh), I thought someone dosed me by putting an illicit substance into my chai, I was so high and out of body. The phenomenal world grew increasingly permeable, and my spirit was lighter than a kite; my soul wanted to fly, far away into another dimension.

Grief rattled me to the core. The hardest part was the fact that hardly anyone could relate or offer meaningful condolences. So-called "spiritual people" would try to tell me I had no reason to be sad, that my guru would always be with me. That didn't help at all—I was still human, for crying out loud. I still felt feelings! I peered into spiritual texts to see if any sages or students had written or spoken of what happens when a guru dies. I found a couple of passages, and I clung to those with all my might.

The first was in the classic Autobiography of a Yogi, when Paramahansa Yogananda loses his master, Sri Yukteshwar. Yogananda cries the entire river Ganges that he'll never behold his beloved teacher in person again.

The second comfort was the story of Ananda, most devoted servant of the Buddha, who felt his sorrow so deeply the night Gautama the Buddha took mahasamadhi that he became enlightened through the sheer force of grief piercing his very heart.

A few expat friends urged me to discuss Ramesh's death with other disciples, that surely the sangha (spiritual fellowship) would lend support, surely they would understand. I found talking to fellow students, in my case, less than comforting. Whether others were deferring their grief or processing it differently (likely), in those I spoke with, there seemed to be a rationalizing of the process, such that because one intellectually knows that nothing is born and nothing dies, particularly the mind of an enlightened being, that there should be nothing to cry about.

Nothing could be further from the truth.

The force of our emotions is the very stuff of life, whether grief, joy, ecstasy, laughter, or even anger. My quaking sobs affirmed that I was ALIVE, damn it. I could feel. I have a vital, awakened heart that can be penetrated and touched, affected to the core.

Intellectualizing or bypassing the emotions, which live in our bodies where we can feel them, is a missed opportunity to experience the rapture of pure existence, which can only be experienced in duality, directly, in the physical body, in the here and now.

It is through our grief that we realize how much we LOVE.

On Love and Loss
Konkan Coast
November 24, 2009

Grief is a difficult emotion to write about. It seems so much easier to write about love. Even writing about anger or sadness seems easier.

I can't put my thoughts together. I keep waiting for the day I wake up and something will feel semi-normal.

But it's not happening.

Instead, I feel more constricted and alone in my grief. I know there must be a few people who are ready to hear it, who can hold me through the tears. It's just so hard to know how to reach out, and how to receive.

How do I know this is the emotion called grief? How do I know it's different than mourning, depression, or mere clinging to the past?

It's because it feels different. Grief just feels *different*. And I've been here before—a few times. I've been through something called D-I-V-O-R-C-E, and I know this profound loss holds a similar emotion.

My first marriage was monumental, even though the relationship only lasted seven years and the legal marriage was short. It was the *real*-ationship and male-female partnership where I'd felt completely myself, for better or for worse. We were truly friends, and I trusted my husband with full exposure.

When the Tower came crashing down at the end of our marriage, I knew it was Life acting through Death, that we were being sent in separate directions in order to keep growing, evolving—and we could not do it together.

With absolute certainty, I knew it was for the Highest Good of All Concerned for my marriage to end. No matter if it was the right thing: even if you know it's gotta go, it's like losing an arm. Needless to say, it hurts like hell.

Post-divorce, it took a good year for the most wrenching, intense waves of grief to quell. I was working a super intense job at the time, one in which I had to be "on" with a happy face every day. It was evenings and weekends that I'd sit on my balcony overlooking the San Francisco skyline, slowly puffing one cigarette, feeling the ache of the let-go of my married life, the departure of the dream, the passing of an intense love relationship.

And yet, and still, it hurt like a mother. It hurt so bad, and I'd cry and cry and cry. I never once "wanted him back." I did wish for his—and of course, my own—ultimate peace and happiness. I knew the past was the past, and it was clearly over. Sure, nostalgia arose: the missing of joyful times, like cross-country skiing in the winter, pancake breakfasts in bed and making love on Sunday mornings, having someone to spoon with. Having someone to sing with, to cook for. Someone to have on your team.

It took about two more years for me to stop wondering how the ex was getting on. Slowly, new life entered the fold. The ex got remarried, rapidly, and had children before I'd even had a proper date, let alone anything resembling a boyfriend.

I went off to India, Europe, New York City, grad school, and the cosmos, refilling my coffers with adventure, passion, growth—and, eventually, boyfriends, too.

Slowly, slowly, over the course of the next several years, I forgot about my ex-husband, though I never stopped being grateful for the seven years we shared together.

But I was talking about grief, wasn't I?

I brought up *Le Divorce* because it evokes the memory that "I've felt this emotion before," and it's here now, again. It is real, and I need to write about it.

Let It Flow
Konkan Coast
November 25, 2009

How does grief feel?
Far beyond sadness, far from depression or general malaise.
Think of words like "wretched."
Wrenching. Tearing. Opening. Wreaking. Wrecking. Racking.
Sobs of sorrow that arise like a tumult of thunder, piercing the heart.
A small baby in sincere pain—raw, egoless pain—crying for the warmth of its mama's breast.
Earthquakes.
A quivering lower lip.
A cavalcade of tears dripping continuously down the cheeks, into the nose.
A wail. A whole body shivering with energy, with emotion, with release.
A loss of appetite. A loss of joy. A loss.
Yes, a loss. It is a Death.
Then, there is the anger. Anger arises because there feels to be no tenderness, no understanding, no arms to comfort.
Because most people haven't had the experience of having a guru-master in the first place, let alone having one die, people tend to not

know how to respond to my grief. I've heard some harsh comments over the past two months, for example:

1. "Haven't you had anyone die before?"

Like that would make it easier! The fact is, NO, I've never had anyone so close to me die before. And even if I had lost a sister, a mother, a brother, my father, a child, would that conceivably make it less painful?

2. "You are being selfish for grieving."

What the...? Selfish because my heart is broken and I'm in pain?

The same person said, "You should be so happy for your Teacher going, since you know he was in physical pain." C'mon here—set aside rationality and let me have my pain! It's become so clear to me that the tears of the survivors are not about *the one who died* (they surely are fine!). The tears are the human emotion experienced by those who are still living for their own loss.

Grief is a passing feeling, and I know Time will heal and transform, but it does not help to minimize it. I loved Ramesh, and we did have an intense closeness at the end. It wasn't more close or less close than any other student. That's each person's experience. I'm saying I loved him, and his death is showing me just how deep that love goes.

3. "I don't want any gurus near me."

Or "A guru is for people who need a father figure."

Or "You don't need a guru anyway."

Sheer ignorance. First of all, unless you've had a guru relationship, you can't possibly know or judge.

4. "Still?" was one person's reaction when I mentioned I was grieving. This was a few short weeks after he died.

I know the Guru is within, that the impersonal Guru has entered my heart, and it is firmly lodged there. But it doesn't mean that in this real-time experience, I don't have pain of loss to heal from. The heart takes its own time.

5. "He would have been disappointed in you."

A few days ago, sitting in a cafe, I noticed an Aussie bloke reading a book by my grand-guru, Sri Nisargadatta Maharaj. I saw the book sitting there, and I knew I was risking it by opening my mouth:

"Oh, you're reading a book by my Teacher's teacher," I said, grasping for a bit of connection, feeling vulnerable.

The guy replied, "Ah, Ram Balsekar," cheekily giving Ramesh a nickname.

"Yes, Ramesh was my Teacher. I miss him. I'm still integrating his death. I miss him still."

The Aussie replied, "He would have been disappointed in you. He spent his life teaching there is no individual. He would have been disappointed in you because you missed the point."

What a jerk. He has no idea what it means to love.

Screw all the intellectual understanding. I'm still in the body, I'm still human, and even if I know the Truth of impermanence, I still have human emotion. Screw your judgment, that I'm attached. Screw all of your concepts.

When Ramesh was still alive, tears arose when speaking of his own guru, and tears arose upon mention of his own son who had passed. "It happened," Ramesh said.

Even with total understanding of impermanence and no separation, emotions happen.

Emotions arise. Joy arises. Sadness arises. Anger arises.

And grief...

Arises.

Let It Flow.

How a Sage Grieves
Konkan Coast
November 26, 2009

By the grace of the Guru, I came across the following passage in my Teacher's book, *It So Happened That: The Unique Teaching of Ramesh S. Balsekar*:

Ramesh writes on loss and death:

A friend of mine lost his wife after fifty-five years of marriage. When I went to see him after ten or twelve days, he was again overcome with feelings. And he had the idea that he had the Understanding, that he knew what It was all about. He had been reading books for forty years.

So he told me, "All that reading, all that knowledge of forty years was found useless when the chips were down." When his wife died he was overcome with grief, and every time someone came to sympathize with him the emotions overwhelmed him again. He said, "Now, when you have come, it is still there, after nearly two weeks. And I thought I was a jnani [an enlightened sage]. I thought I had understood."

At that time to speak to him on this matter would have been to add insult to injury. So I didn't speak to him then. But when I went home, somehow I went straight to my desk and wrote him a longish letter. I concluded by saying, "I presume you have read this. Please forgive the impertinence, and just throw it away."

But I wrote because it was almost compulsive. What I wrote to him was this: "Your reaction to the death of your wife was a perfectly normal reaction for the body-mind organism in question. You love your wife; you miss your wife. That's all there is. So the reaction to the death of your wife is perfectly natural, perfectly spontaneous. What is perhaps wrong is your re-action to that reaction. You are reacting to that reaction saying, 'I thought I was a jnani and here I am groveling in grief.' So that reaction is what is incorrect." And that reaction really proves that his understanding was not deep enough.

So I wrote and said, "If you had not loved your wife as much as you did, then probably her death would not have affected you as much. And then you probably would have thought, 'I know what it's all about. I am a jnani. The death of my wife doesn't mean so much. I accept it.' But that reaction would not have been because of being a jnani, it would have been because you didn't love your wife!"

Exactly what I needed to hear.

The Power of Love
Konkan Coast
November 28, 2009

HOW DOES THIS GRIEF FEEL?

In the last weeks, I've been in a lot of pain—a void, a loss, a transformation. There are a lot of feelings around being alone in this grief. Sometimes anger arises—at no one in particular; it's just there. I've had unexplainable moments of bliss, ecstasy as well. Whether or not they're related, I don't know. I just feel really open and raw.

I had to undertake a strict health recovery program, which I'm still on. This means I've had to put myself on a more regular eating and sleeping schedule. Going through intense grief is a transformation that requires a huge amount of energy. It is totally disorienting, and eventually calls for an attempt at finding a new rhythm so the body systems don't get totally whacked out, which happened to me anyway.

I don't feel ready to socialize much—it's hard to socialize when you're unsure if you're going to cry or blurt anger or get ecstatically high all in the same conversation. Better to be alone... but it does feel like I need my friends to know what I'm dealing with.

On top of the heartbreak of death, I had three severe slips and falls in the month after his death. I got the message that I really have had to take extra good care of myself. It appears that physical accidents occur more regularly to those who are grieving. This could be attributed to not being grounded, the soul wanting to follow the person who has died or left. It can also be attributed to the body taking on some of the emotional pain through "accidents."

Some folks have said, why don't you talk to your other *sangha* members (fellow students) to share your grief? Well, just because someone was or is a disciple does not mean they are in the same place as I am. Maybe they aren't as sensitive. Maybe they are distracting themselves.

One fellow student told me to "just stay really busy," which is good advice, but the truth is, I need to express myself. Whether anyone listens, or cares, or feels some of the same feelings, doesn't matter. I just need to give myself the space to grieve, and *maybe* I'll get some comfort or reprieve by releasing it.

While I do spontaneously remember satsangs and moments of laughter, realization, and intensity of experiencing Ramesh in the flesh, the grief is different than merely losing the person. The grief is also about the passing of a phase of my life—a chapter—in which I was a disciple. A devoted one filled with bhakti. A period of time in which I'd flown faster than the speed of light across the world, guided by the power of love and devotion, to express my gratitude and respect to this Master.

I endured some scary, scary shit in Mumbai to be near him—being strong and tough all the time as a solo woman traveler and the events surrounding the Bombay terrorist attacks of November 2008. And I spent one of the hardest travel months of my life in June 2009, with no air-conditioning and the monsoon delayed three weeks. I felt I would explode from shakti and tapas, humidity and tension, but I knew that THIS WAS IT. These were the final days, the final talks with Ramesh, and I was determined to stay close as long as I could.

These memories, and many more, are in me. They are being alchemized, transmuted. They are in my blood, my bones, and more than "spirituality," "enlightenment," "realization," or "Advaita" (non-duality), to me, Ramesh, in the end, evoked in me the Power of Love.

The Power of Love will take you to the Moon and back. The Power of Love will show you a strength you never knew existed. And the Power of Love is what makes miracles manifest.

The amazing thing about the Power of Love is that it cannot be manufactured. You can't put it on your credit card. You can't "do" anything, for Love does it, *to* you and *through* you.

Thank God for the perfect Guru, the perfect mirror. Thank you for this experience, for this fulfillment of seeking. I trust You, God, that the tears will end in Your time, not mine.

As the tears barrel down my cheeks...

I LOVE.

PART IV
Life After Death

Transitioning

In the months following Ramesh's passing, I attempted to continue on with life in India, but things were not the same. I knew this long chapter of my life was coming to a close. I no longer had a need to stay within a day's journey to Mumbai. I struggled to make a life as a temporary expat in a small, coastal village in Karnataka, South India. As a writer and introvert, I still spend most of my time alone; but even writers and introverts need some human contact. I found that I was caught between worlds. I couldn't totally relate to Western travelers anymore, and I couldn't fully integrate into local Indian life, either. It was time to make a shift. The spiritual seeking was finished, my Guru was no longer in the body, I had enough travel writing material to last a lifetime, and I had no need to vagabond through South Asia. Would I return to the States? It would take a while to get my psyche prepared to return to the West.

It was about "timepassing until God makes up his or her mind," as Ramesh had said about whether full realization, aka enlightenment, would occur in one wherein the seeking had stopped. While I let Life show me the way, I used the time best I could and completed a traditional Indian yoga teacher training program in Bangalore, Karnataka. This intensive program was not focused solely on asana, the physical practice of yoga. Rather, it emphasized the other branches of yoga, including jnana, bhakti, raja, and karma.

In the spring of 2010, after completing the yoga certification, I traveled onward to Tiruvannamalai in Tamil Nadu, to reside at a small ashram at the base of the holy mountain of Arunachala, the home of Sri Ramana Maharshi, the great Advaita sage. I had no interest in staying anywhere besides ashrams at that point. I had no interest in being part of a traveler scene. I wanted only a spiritual vibration, solitude, and security to relax as a solo woman. And even though there was no more seeking or suffering left, I continued to love the religious culture, rituals, and devotional practices of India...

Tapasya
Tiruvannamalai
April 1, 2010

By local bus from Bangalore, I rumbled into Tiruvannamalai, Tamil Nadu, located about four hours southwest of Chennai, where Shiva dwells as the red-earth mountain, holy Arunachala. It's my third visit here over the past four years. I've come here to deepen my connection to the Self, the Source, through meditation, contemplation, and yogasana.

This is where the Great Sage of Arunachala, Bhagavan Sri Ramana Maharshi, transmitted his monumental teachings from 1896 until his death in 1950. Today, the *Ramanasramam* (Sri Ramana Ashram in the local language of Tamil) is thriving at the base of the mountain.

For about a month, I'm staying in a small, private affiliate ashram devoted to Ramana; then, for the last ten days of April, I have a reservation in the main ashram. Let's see if I can last that long. It's hotter here than any place I've been during India's infamous hot season. Right now, it seems even hotter than Varanasi, where I could fry an egg on my balcony. It's definitely hotter than pre-monsoon Mumbai, where at least the occasional lapping of the ocean breeze teased me with the promise of cooling down. There's no breeze here. It's dry as a bone. But I need to be here: it's off-season, it's quiet, and I can concentrate on *sadhana*, or practice.

I enjoy India most in places and seasons where tourists are few and far between. This means being willing to go off the beaten path—and then, being willing to tread even further. This also means enduring scorching heat or monsoon deluges for days. If one can adjust to the climate, with mental fortitude, the experience is usually filled with internal rewards.

I may be crazy. Sometimes I wonder about my undertakings. But there's something in yogic philosophy called "tapas" that makes sense to me. *Tapas*, meaning austerity or discipline, also means heat. Tapas is one of the foundational prongs of Patanjali's yoga sutras called *niyama*, wherein the *sadhaka* (practitioner) embraces a personal code of discipline to strengthen her yoga path.

In *Great Swan: Meetings with Ramakrishna*, Lex Hixon describes *Tapasya* as "the inner discipline that generates heat and intensity throughout the subtle nervous system" and "the practice that awakens the upward-flowing energy of realization." Sitting with intention in an otherwise unbearably hot climate in order to have uninterrupted time with the Source is a perfect example of tapasya.

Another example of tapas is the month I spent in Mumbai in the pre-monsoon scorching heat in order to attend the last daily satsang talks of my Guru before he left his body: it was insanely hot, I couldn't afford A/C, the body was miserable, the brain was cooking, but the heart was soaring in love and gratitude.

Was it worth it? You better believe it.

Ashram Dweller
Tiruvannamalai
April 3, 2010

It came to me while chanting the one hundred and eight names of Ramana Maharshi during the morning prayers that this could be a good time to write more regularly again as part of my spiritual practice. It also gives a nice focus to the day. And so I will.

The ashram where I am staying is very small, immaculately clean. I've come so far from the Erin before who used to hate ashram life. Actually, I realize now I didn't hate ashram life: I hated being herded around in cases where it was a tourist-oriented ashram. Now, when the focus is serious meditation and contemplation, and noble silence is being practiced—well, I'm like a duck in water. (If only there was a pond. In these temperatures, I'd be soaking in it.)

There are several babas and swamis here, and they are in silence unless it is necessary to speak. The food here is heavy, rice-based, and delicious. I need to watch my intake: I'm slowly growing a baba-belly since the thirty days at the yoga university had the same starchy cuisine. I'm not used to being fed three times a day. I think I'm the only person at the yoga instructor's course that actually gained weight.

One Indian baba here at the ashram has such a wild look, I won't even peek in his direction as we sit down on the floor to eat our meals. He's probably harmless, but he's got the mad look of a crazed warrior god, with long matted white hair and three huge Jatas—one sprouting straight from the top of his head and one growing out from each temple. While eating, he ties them up in a top knot bun. With the smearing of *vibhuti* (sacred white-gray ash) on his forehead, the red *tilak* in the center of his third eye, and his "I've just seen Shiva in the form of a ghost" look in his permanently widened eyes, he looks like he could jump off a cliff any moment into maha-nirvana.

The first morning at the ashram, I woke up at 3:30 a.m. without the alarm, soaked in sweat, of course. I read a bit from a Ramana book, bathed, and practiced yogasana and pranayama. I also chanted a bit—it's great to be in an ashram where you can chant openly in the wee hours of the dawn without feeling like you're disturbing others. The yoga course really renewed my love of chanting, and I've come to understand more Sanskrit and pronunciation, especially through our daily recitations of the Bhagavad Gita. In the morning and evenings, we chanted the following Santi Mantra with great gusto, and chills ran down my spine:

> *Om asato maa sadgamaya*
> *Tamaso maa jyotirgamaya*
> *Mrtyor ma amrtangamaya*
> *Om Santih Santih Santih*

Let us move from unreality to reality, from darkness to light, and from mortality to immortality. Om peace, peace, peace.

> *Sarve bhavantu sukhinah*
> *Sarve santu niramayah*
> *Sarve bhadrani pasyantu*
> *Maa kascit duhkhabhag bhavet*
> *Om Santih Santih Santih*

May all be happy. May all be free from disabilities. May all look to the good of others. May none be subjected to misery. Om peace, peace, peace.

After completing my personal practice, I joined the swamis and babas and the four foreign guests in the prayer room for further chanting from 6:30 to 8:00 a.m. When the head Swamiji began chanting the one hundred and eight names of Ramana Maharshi and adorning the small *murti* (idol) with hundreds of white, red, pink, and yellow blossoms, I was suddenly overcome with tears. I was feeling the love and bhakti for Ramesh, who was a lifelong devotee of Ramana.

It's been just over six months since Ramesh's passing. Of course, I know he is always with me, everywhere, and the Guru in my Heart is here and now; still, the human part of me does miss my Teacher. I think of the precious moments absorbed in the Truth while perched at his feet, and I know I'm extremely lucky to have encountered him. From what I've read from great bhaktas, that very ache for the Teacher is the connection to God and Self (which are the same), and is really the whole point—that is what it is all about. That very ache *is* the Source.

So, it's a bittersweet, happy-sad feeling that wells up in my chest—that Divine Love.

It's a pleasure-pain that one can actually enjoy, this bliss of tenderness.

Earth Changes
Tiruvannamalai
April 5, 2010

I woke up late.

It was 5:30 a.m.

Like I said, late—for an ashram.

Skipped yoga, read a book on Ramana Maharshi's teaching, bathed and scurried off for prayers in the meditation hall.

After prayers and typing up the previous day's notes, I started the day by visiting the ashram of a local woman saint, Sri Siva Sakthi Ammaiyer, who has been in *mouni* (silence) for years. Every morning, there is a darshan with Maa for only fifteen minutes. Visitors arrive early to meditate and bask in the healing vibrations of the darshan room before she enters. I came here once before, and the same thing happened to me again today: I closed my eyes to meditate and enter the silence, feeling the energies in the potently charged room. It's like being in a Reiki tunnel. Without opening my eyes, I became aware of an electromagnetic buzzing and heightened awareness. I wondered whether Maa had entered the room—she walks and moves completely silently. Indeed, when I opened my eyes, she'd entered the hall and was slowly moving toward her chair in the center.

Maa sits for a while in her seat, then stands and moves about the room, making eye contact with some while glancing in an indirect manner above others' heads. Sometimes, she makes tiny, barely perceptible movements with her hands in a sort of mudra. As an intuitive myself, I can feel what she's doing—she's directing with and working with healing energy. It is as if her work in life—her job—is to stay connected to the Source through silence, prayer, and meditation; then, she transmits that pure awareness toward others in her presence. The gift of awareness is that it goes exactly where it needs to go to heal—no mental effort is needed.

"Quite an imagination you have," one might say. Well, it's just like going to the doctor. Some of us go to energy healers.

Whatever works, you know.

On the way out of the darshan hall, I noticed a typed, channeled message from Maa posted on the wall, from December 2009. The gist of the message was that over the past year, the earth's rotation has speeded up slightly, but with great impact, due to the karma of individuals. This is the cause of the great climate changes and natural disasters. This speeding up will continue gradually but more intensely through 2012—more earthquakes, tsunamis, floods, volcanic activity, and the like will occur. People in coastal areas or on islands should be careful. India may be less affected than other places. The message stated that aware individuals need to strengthen and stabilize their inner peace and patience in order to weather (no pun intended) the coming changes.

It's possible that awareness of the upcoming (and recent) global calamities is what has led me to learn to live as simply as possible—or maybe, I just like it. I've learned I can be happy (and, in fact, happier) with very few possessions and no expectations. I've learned that less distraction and less complexity in my daily life help me be calmer and focus on maintaining inner silence *no matter what is happening* on the outside.

This is also found in the simplicity of food choices. Perhaps, if the world is going to go through a massive geological shift, and it gets to a point where food is hard to get (food that is costly in terms of resources to produce), people will need to learn to subsist on a simple vegetarian diet. So, perhaps unconsciously I've begun training the body-mind, à la Frances Moore Lappe's pivotal 1971 book on simpler food choices, *Diet for a Small Planet.*

My own digestive system works like a charm on a plant-based South Indian diet. I rarely ever have any health problems like colds or flu, indigestion or constipation. It took a while to adjust to this sort of eating—the changes in spices and protein expectations. It also took a while to let go of the idea that there has to be constant variety in the menu, like "Sushi on Saturday, burritos on Tuesday, Chinese on Thursday, and Italian on Friday." I've found that my own body actually responds better to a diet with simple, rather than extreme, fluctuations in rhythm. And you wouldn't believe the savings in food costs.

Progress not perfection, however! I'm an *effortless*-effort kind of person. Things go and things change when they're meant to, and not one moment before. Awareness is the only efforting, so to speak—and that's probably ninety-nine percent of any change.

Now, let's see when coffee leaves me. *Sigh...* One of the last little indulgent luxuries. In the meantime, until it goes, I'll enjoy right now... with awareness.

S-l-u-u-u-u-r-p!

Daily Bread
Tiruvannamalai
April 10, 2010

Yesterday afternoon, I was so touched and happy to be in my little ashram when I witnessed the following scene:

I emerged from my room just as the sun decided to cool it a bit—at 5 p.m.—to take chai and prepare to head to the main Ramana ashram for evening meditation and chanting.

Just before exiting, at the gates of my ashram, about thirty babas were lined up with round, steel tiffin meal containers in hand. Their other hands held a walking staff, as was typical. All of their possessions dangled from their "baba bag"—a single shoulder bag, and they were dressed in bright ochre robes, the color of the burning sunset.

Most appeared to be in their fifties or sixties, with shortly cropped gray hair and closely trimmed beards—a few younger renunciates wore coal-black, dusty dreadlocks. The former were most certainly sannyasins who were living off alms and pursuing only spiritual goals after completing their householder phase of life.

It suddenly hit me that it was Saturday, of course—known as "beggars' day" throughout India—and our little ashram was doing its part to support the spiritual renunciates. Standing on the steps, the white-clad Mother of our ashram was preparing to serve these men—poor in possessions but rich in spirit. Ma was stirring a mammoth-sized vessel of delicious-smelling curd rice, seasoned with fragrant curry leaves. The silent babas emanated contentment as they lined up for Ma's generous ladle.

I walked past the scene swiftly so as not to draw attention to myself, and my heart opened for joy. What a small thing—to offer a few cups of yogurt and grain. And what a large blessing—to fill so many bellies, supporting these men in their commitment to the Divine.

Sannyasins are, in a sense, preparing for the ultimate samadhi known as Death. Learning to live without fear is of key importance. When one knows it is possible to live with nothing, what is there to fear in Nothingness?

All That You Can't Leave Behind
Tiruvannamalai
April 15, 2010

The only baggage you can bring
Is all that you can't leave behind
– U2

One thing about being a traveling yogi-gypsy without a permanent abode is that it is impossible to hold on to books for the simple reason I can't possibly carry more than one or two. As it is, I'm bearing the weight of my entire belongings every time I move from one location to the next. It seems the laptop and its accessories are meant to be in my possession lately for writing and preparing astrology readings, and that is a significant weight. Everything I need in life, from any and all critical paperwork to notebooks to yoga mat, has to be borne on my own back.

I fantasize about having a personal Sherpa, or a porter, like days of old—like a traveling lady of colonial times with a few trunks and a hefty wallah to carry them. I don't naturally pack light, and it is not fun lugging my heavy bag on buses and trains. Destiny's hand has dealt me a solo spiritual journey for the time being—so I keep paring down, paring down, paring down. The funny thing is, material items constantly come my way: other travelers pass an item on to me; I'm given a gift of remembrance; I find a small stone that wants to stay with me; I somehow end up with five skin creams (yes, I'm a vagabond, but I'm a woman, too).

And so, and so... I keep letting go, letting go, letting go.

For me, this is partly about the principle of *aparigraha*, meaning non-covetousness, non-hoarding, or non-possession.

Aparigraha is one of the five *yamas*, the social disciplines that form the first rung of the raja yoga path as put forth by sage Patanjali in the Yoga Sutras. Actually, aparigraha came naturally to me, long before I knew who Patanjali was. It's been a process, both consciously and unconsciously, of relinquishing possessions over the past ten years. Constantly letting go and decluttering, keeping things as simple as possible, helps me to keep my mind clear and to see what's really important. It also gives me tremendous freedom to be guided from one moment to the next.

Books are the hardest thing to release. I constantly have to recycle and sell them—even when they touch me so deeply as to blow my mind, or blow my heart open, as the case may be. The hardest surrendering of texts has been when I've had to recycle those written by Ramesh. I've read probably twenty books by him, and they are all precious. A few of them have chilled me to the very core.

When I moved from my seasonal house near the beach this winter, I had to recycle all of my texts in order to keep only that which I could carry. Since Ramesh is no longer here in the body, I could hardly believe I had the ability to give away the books he'd written. Yet, I couldn't justify carrying them with me; I couldn't physically do it anyway. And, since I never know where I'm going next, where would I send them if I were to post them? I had to assure myself that his books, so long as they're in print, could be purchased again. In addition, since I was handing them over to a worthy bookseller in the village, I knew that another person would benefit greatly by having access to these gems. I told myself that I'd absorbed the words into my own Heart and that the most important points were a part of my being. I miss those books like I miss my dearest friends.

I made another huge step in aparigraha this year when I burned a whole year's worth of journals—they'd been partially in my possession and partly left in storage in a guest house in South India. Up to now, journals have been my main material attachment on the road and back in the States. I've been keeping journals for twenty-seven years of my life! That's a lot of writing!

I have four massive crates of journals in a friend's cellar in California. Those crates comprise almost all the items that I have left in the West. I've been wondering for the past three years when and if I'd be ready to say goodbye to those. "But there's such good writing in there!" "It's all good fodder for my books later!" "What about leaving a legacy?" "I'll want to read about my adventures again someday!" "I'll have time to read them aloud when I'm an old lady in a rocking chair!"

Good points, indeed. But it seems my particular flavor of spiritual journey in this life is a bit extreme: I get to see what it's like to be completely unattached to the past. I'm not going halfway up the mountain—I'm climbing Everest, it seems, and alone at that—for the time being.

And so, I created a pyre outside my temporary little abode near the beach and said goodbye to those ten journals chock-full of memories. Before burning them, I skimmed them and, I admit, I was awed by my own experiences. But I know beyond the shadow of a doubt that more experiences, more words, and more wonder are around every single corner of my life, every single day. I could not carry those journals with me. I trusted that the wisdom was a part of my very being, and that I'd be able to recall, write, and speak about the most important incidences of the past when necessary. I did tear out a few important notes and short story drafts before succumbing the notebooks to the flames.

To Renounce or Not to Renounce
Tiruvannamalai
April 16, 2010

The path of renunciation isn't for everyone. The Truth is, even though my present path is about traveling as light as possible, I feel that those who maintain worldly lives, careers, families, and marriages with peace and harmony are the real spiritual masters!

Yesterday, I spent a marvelous day (O blessed, cooling cloud cover of great relief!) hiking on the holy mountain of Arunachala and meditating in Virupaksha Cave, where Sri Ramana Maharshi lived for seventeen years.

Sitting outside the cave after meditating, I read a chapter from the book *Ramana Maharshi and the Path of Self-Knowledge* by Arthur Osborne, a Western devotee who first met Sri Ramana in 1945. Not coincidentally, the chapter referred to householder life versus sannyasin, or renunciate, life. Bhagavan Sri Ramana discouraged devotees from giving up householder life unless the pull from within was natural, i.e., *an unavoidable internal thrust*. It's not about being homeless in order to be spiritual. The point is that "true renunciation is in the mind and is neither achieved by physical renunciation nor impeded by the lack of it."

Here's an excerpt:

Devotee: I am inclined to give up my job and remain always with Sri Bhagavan.

Bhagavan Sri Ramana Maharshi: Bhagavan is always with you, in you. The Self in you is Bhagavan. It is that you should realize.

D: But I feel the urge to give up all attachments and renounce the world as a sannyasin.

B: Renunciation does not mean outward divestment of clothes and so on or abandonment of home. *True renunciation is the renunciation of desires, passions, and attachments* [emphasis added].

D: But single-minded devotion to God may not be possible unless one leaves the world.

B: No; one who truly renounces actually merges in the world and expands his love to embrace the whole world. It would be more correct to describe the attitude of the devotee as universal love than as abandoning home to don the ochre robe.

D: At home the bonds of affection are too strong.

B: He who renounces when he is not yet ripe for it only creates new bonds.

D: Is not renunciation the supreme means of breaking attachments?

B: It may be so for one whose mind is already free from entanglements. But you have not grasped the deeper import of renunciation: great souls who have abandoned the life of the world have done so not out of aversion to family life but because of their large-hearted and all-embracing love for all mankind and all creatures.

D: The family ties will have to go sometime so why shouldn't I take the initiative and break them now so that my love can be equal to all?

B: When you really feel that equal love for all, when your heart has so expanded as to embrace the whole of creation, you will certainly not feel like giving up this or that; you will simply drop off from secular life as a ripe fruit does from the branch of a tree. You will feel that the whole world is your home. The one obstacle is the mind and it must be overcome whether in the home or the jungle. If you can do it in the jungle why not in the home? Therefore why change the environment? Your efforts can be made even now, whatever be the environment.

Every journey is truly unique...

Living Is Life's Only Purpose
Tiruvannamalai
April 17, 2010

There is no question of failure, neither in the short run nor in the long. It is like traveling a long and arduous road in an unknown country. Of all the innumerable steps, there is only the last which brings you to your destination. Yet you will consider all previous steps as failures. Each brought you nearer to your goal, even when you had to turn back to bypass an obstacle. In reality, each step brings you to your goal, because to be always on the move—learning, discovering, unfolding—is your eternal destiny.

Living is life's only purpose. The Self does not identify itself with success or failure—the very idea of becoming this or that is unthinkable. The Self understands that success and failure are relative and related, that they are the very warp and weft of life. Learn from both and go beyond. If you have not learnt, repeat.

~ Sri Nisargadatta Maharaj, *I Am That*

Sri Nisargadatta Maharaj (April 17, 1897 - September 8, 1981) is an Advaita sage from Bombay. He was my Teacher's direct Guru, so that makes him my "grand-guru." I'm so happy I'm a part of his lineage, because he was an embodiment of fierce grace. Plus, his story is unconventional—on the surface, nothing special, and that's what makes it so special.

Nisargadatta (meaning "given by the natural state") Maharaj ("great king") lived in a dodgy part of town, close to the red-light district. In fact, unbeknownst to me until later, the very first night I landed in Mumbai, I actually stayed in a cheap hotel that not-coincidentally lay just around the corner from his family house!

Nisargadatta was a simple shopkeeper. He was a corner bidi wallah— he sold hand-rolled cigarettes and other various items in a local corner kiosk. He smoked. He ate meat. He had a family. And he was wide awake.

Nisargadatta was largely illiterate. He wasn't a scholar of the scriptures. He did love bhajans, however, and continued to sing and revel in the music of the Divine until his end. The story goes that Maharaj awakened pretty much on the spot after a friend brought him to a Bombay master, Sri Siddharameshwar Maharaj (1888 – 1936). The guru told Nisargadatta that all he needed to do was unwaveringly remember that his true nature was the Entire Universe—Brahman. Nisargadatta, with his simple nature and uncomplicated mind, clung to that truth with all his might and all his being. As a result, without any *sadhana* (spiritual practice) besides total faith and trust, he merged into complete Oneness and absolute realization.

Over the years, Nisargadatta continued his householder duties and maintained his cigarette shop, but in a totally nonattached manner. He still conducted the same actions as before—he never gave up bidis or meat, stating that, "Yes, the body has retained some habits." But now, the true knowledge of jñana was the constant flow. All sense of personal doer-ship had been uprooted. Nisargadatta was fully immersed in Consciousness. The ego had been reduced to a speck—just enough to keep the personality on the planet.

His personality is one of his claims to fame in the spiritual hall of sages: Nisargadatta is known for his angry outbursts and unpredictable spouts. If anger was necessary to drive a point home to a disciple, he wouldn't mince words. The thing is, he was fully unattached: as soon as the point was made, full release of the anger also happened, just as quickly as it came. He might laugh at a disciple's joke in the very next instant. This is because "no one was there"—there was absolutely no involvement or identification. He was a true *Guñātita* (one who is beyond the three gunas, or primal urges), flowing like water between *tamas*, *rajas*, and *sattva* qualities. This dispels the illusion that a sage must exhibit a particular behavior to be a sage: a true sage is beyond qualification.

Nisargadatta was as natural as an ocean that ranges from placid to torrential, depending on the energies afoot.

I Am That: Conversations with Sri Nisargadatta Maharaj is mind-blowing, and is known as a modern spiritual classic. I first came across this book in Rishikesh in 2002, my first visit to India. At the time, it went right over my head. I couldn't understand it at all. It took several trips down the non-dual rabbit hole and a bit more spiritual maturing before I'd be able to absorb the teachings therein. After I met Ramesh, I got "it"—"it" meaning an intellectual understanding of nonduality—and then, Nisargadatta's words flowed like sheer poetry.

I used to read one of the short chapters in *I Am That* each morning, sitting on my balcony in South India, birds chirping as the sun rose. Sometimes, tears would stream down my face as my heart opened with awareness. It's impossible to put the absolute truth of consciousness into words. This is why poets and fantasy writers and artists are so important: we can understand the Truth indirectly. It's like the Buddha said when it comes to teachings, "The finger pointing at the Moon is not the Moon," but it at least shows us the way.

Ultimately, we have to experience it directly, for ourselves, and in the Heart. Usually, if the experience brings you to tears of joy or—in some cases—bittersweet pain, you've hit the right spot.

Inquiring Minds Want to Know
Tiruvannamalai
April 19, 2010

Last night, I experienced a deep meditation at one of the meditation halls in the main Ramana ashram.

At first, I noticed I was getting frustrated—I couldn't concentrate on a single subject, known as *dharana*; I couldn't settle on the "I." I almost quit and went back to my room because, as I've said before, I'm an *effortless*-effort kind of person. If it's not happening naturally, I'm not into it. Yet, as much as I dislike forced practice, I'm also a person who enjoys a challenge. Instead of sitting there mulling over the fact that no practices are ultimately necessary, I decided to try the practice of *vichara*, Sri Ramana Maharshi's recommended practice of self-inquiry.

All methods are totally unnecessary if one is merely able to give up the idea of a separate, individual self functioning through the body-mind. If a person accepts that wholly and completely, 100 percent, then there is no need for methods.

For all the other humans who still feel they must *do* something in order to realize the Self, Ramana recommended either *vichara* (self-inquiry) or total surrender to the Divine—a surrender that stretches beyond a subject-object relation with the Source. Regarding the latter, "For such self-surrender to be effective one must have no will or desire of one's own and one must be completely free of the idea that there is an individual person who is capable of acting independently of God," writes scholar David Godman in *Be As You Are: The Teachings of Sri Ramana Maharshi*.

Personally, I'm of the "surrender" variety. Raising the white flag to the Divine is just fine with me. I've realized that I'm powerless over everything, anyway. "Thy will be done." Whether I think I'm doing something or building something or free-willing anything, the truth is that Cosmic Law is in charge, "from raising a little finger to an earthquake," as my Teacher used to say.

So, I'm surrendered. You got me, God.

Yet while I'm still living the rest of this life, I'm open to trying different things.

So, I attempted to go deeper through the other route: vichara, or "self-inquiry," the practice of "Who am I?" or "Who is this me who is asking the question?" or "Who is it that is observing this thought/experience/pain/pleasure?"

The point is to follow the "I"-thought to the Source, when one realizes that one is actually the subject. If one is the subject, one could never be the object, i.e., one is not the body. Ultimately, the "I" thought is traced to the Self, where there is no separation, because the "I" is the Self. In the most distilled point of Truth, there is no such thing as Self-realization, because the Self is always realized. It's an illusion—maya—that we are somehow individually separate. It's a part of the lila—cosmic play—that enables life as we know it to go on, and that we get to be the experiencers thereof, through identification with our senses and merging with the sense objects.

If this sounds a bit confusing, that's because it is—confusing to the mind—until you try it. The practice of vichara is easy once you observe your Self as an observer. Then, the trick is to keep tracing that observation back until the individual "I" is no longer there—it's just "the I of I," the Source.

This is where *jñana* comes in—jñana being knowledge that brings one closer to the Self. The wisdom in jñana, whether *hearing* the Truth (*sravana*), or seeing it pictorially as a model, or directly experiencing it in any way at all, is that the intellect can be used to apprehend reality. This is a tool—a concept—that can be used to go beyond all concepts. Because the ultimate Truth, being beyond all refutable concepts, cannot be put into words, all talk and all books and all scriptures are like concept-thorns used to pry other concept-thorns out. Once the splinter is out of the foot (or head, as the case may be), one is meant to throw the thorn away. Then, the jñana will begin to flow automatically, deepening and nourishing the seeker, until full merging with the Self occurs, 100 percent. It does not come and go.

Is practice (sadhana) necessary? No, and yes. If practice is necessary, according to an individual's body-mind composition that includes genes and conditioning, a person will practice, through meditation, self-inquiry, purification techniques, yoga, and the like. However, if and when the Truth is fully apprehended—and it drops into one's Heart (meaning, it moves beyond intellectual understanding and into experience), then no practices are necessary—no more seeking, no more sadhana.

If practices continue after the Truth is embodied, then that's just because the sage—the jñani—feels like doing them. Maybe he enjoys meditation; maybe she still digs yogasana. Maybe one person continues working at their law practice, while another simply watches cricket on the telly. It really doesn't matter if one is seated in the Self. "The whole point," Ramesh was fond of saying, "is to relax!"

Knowing all this, how did my one-hour practice of vichara go last evening?

Well enough. I found that self-inquiry and tracing the "I" to its Source helped me to rest in the Truth. By no means did the "me" completely dissolve, yet it became so clear that "I" was the subject, and "I" was happy to sit in that awareness.

That's the point that Ramana advises us to cling to: cling to the "I" until the "I" disappears.

And so there "I" clung for a while—hanging on to my little "I" life-buoy in a deep-blue expanse of awareness.

You are
unconditioned and changeless,
formless and immovable,
unfathomable awareness,
imperturbable:
so hold to nothing but consciousness.
— Sage Ashtavakra
Ashtavakra Gita, Ch.1, v.17

PART V
Awakened Living

The End of Me

*In May 2010, I visited Mumbai once again to honor Ramesh's May 25
birthday with the other devotees—the first jayanti since he had passed. It
took all of my strength to get on a plane to leave India, though I knew it
was time. After a summer in Germany with my family—a necessary few
months' stopover, halfway to America, in order to integrate—I returned to
the United States in the autumn of 2010.*

*It was a rough reentry to the San Francisco Bay Area, but it had to hap-
pen eventually. Being in the States again was like learning to walk and
talk all over again. I spent most of the time alone, in quietude, writing
and compiling my* Bindi Girl *travel tales. I was still grieving Ramesh, and
homesick for India. Some nights, I'd crawl into bed wearing my clothes
from India—a shawl, a tunic, a skirt drenched in memories and the smell
of incense to soothe my heartache.*

*I was still without a permanent residence. I lived as a traveling writer and
semi-renunciate, house- and pet-sitting for long stretches. In between gigs, I'd
visit a retreat center or go camping, and make it work. The seeking was finished; there was nowhere to go and nothing left to do, except to see what would
happen. And, one ordinary day in 2011, about one year and four months after
Ramesh's passing, something did happen: the end of "me." Awakening.*

*Prior to meeting Tim, I had no idea that realization was truly possible or
available to me in this lifetime. It is said in many spiritual traditions from*

the East that you have to hear *a seed of the truth—a form of transmission—directly from an awakened person, personally. And that seed may erupt into a flame!*

This was quite different from the New Age airy-fairy ideas of "attaining enlightenment" that had surrounded me in the 1980s, replete with crystals and aliens and ascended beings living inside Mount Shasta. It was also different than the hip cats I'd learned about as a child in the 1970s, in which I'd need to be an emaciated old yogi in a dirty blanket with matted dreadlocks in India to achieve a blissed-out state of grace. A Perma-High.

Most importantly, it was different than what I'd learned in vipassana meditation, in which I'd have to sit in meditation a minimum of two hours a day for umpteenth lifetimes in order to be liberated. And, I'd have to abstain from many indulgent pleasures, adhere to a strict moral code, and work, work, work my ass off to attain the status of an arhat *(liberated person). God, I grew tired and bored just thinking about it!*

I frankly never KNEW about non-duality and connection to the Self or Source as a direct route to realization. I never knew, until Tim explained it to me, that there was the possibility of apprehending—totally and irrefutably—"What Is" in every instant.

Though I'd studied the self (with small "s") and the Self (with big "S") in my Master's program in Transpersonal Psychology, it is one thing to mentally conceive of the Ground of Being and Existence, and another thing to live the realization. To no longer identify with the small self (the "me"). To clear seeing and direct experiencing that there is no one there to suffer.

The concept of the idea of existing separately as a highly charged "me" thought can dissolve in an instant. In other words, anyone can awaken at any moment. Though the stories of one's experience of awakening are interesting, entertaining, dramatic, and inspiring, they may or may not contain valid pointers. The hows and whens of that happening are as unique as the individual who has awakened...

RAMESH'S GRACE
11:11 P.M.
Sri Ramana Maharshi Ashram
Holy Mountain, Arunachala
Tiruvannamalai

I am dreaming.

I am lucid dreaming, aware it is a dream.

I am also aware I am lying in bed in an ashram in Tiruvannamalai, India—frying hot, with mosquitoes biting my knees and no fan due to power cuts.

I am enjoying the dream. I let it continue.

Besides, in the dream, it is a much more pleasant scene. I am in a sort of "dream satsang" with several devotees of our late Guruji, Ramesh S. Balsekar. I see familiar faces—Suresh, Murthy, several foreigners, Indians. It could be a private home, an ashram or garden atmosphere—but really, we could be anywhere in India. It could be Mumbai, Tiruvannamalai, or even a place in Goa. People at the dream satsang are mingling. Some are dressed in more religious garb, like sannyasins (renunciates), or are wearing traditional Indian dress. Others are totally "worldly."

We have been paying respects to our beloved Master, who is no longer alive. It could be our guru Ramesh's birthday (May 25), or Guru Purnima in July, or even the anniversary of his mahasamadhi (passing of a realized sage), September 27. It could very well be any day at all. We are chitchatting about our Teacher and the Understanding, and enjoying each other's company. Nothing special is happening here, while at the same time, it is all very special.

A wave comes over me, a knowing, that now is a good time to tell my story to the others. It is a bubbling up of joy, gratitude, and happiness. And, to celebrate the brilliance of our beloved Teacher, an Advaita sage whose presentation of his concept of enlightenment was so darn subtle you would miss the sword of the impact if you were not totally alert, aware, and paying full attention.

In the dream satsang, I am excited to share with the other sishyas (disciples) *what happened*. Several straggling visitors leave the event—off they go. A few distracting barking dogs are shooed away in the dream—certainly symbolizing the disruptive element, the doubters and persistent intellectual contrarians, those who could not yet hear a simple truth told from an average woman like me.

"I have to tell you a story!" I announce to my friends, heart beating with joy. "Our Ramesh was so brilliant, the message so clear... and it got the job done! I want to tell you what happened!"

The friends gather round. They want to listen, for they loved Ramesh with all their hearts, too. They are happy to hear my account. A final yapping dog is shooed off over a high fence. One friend lights a cigarette and gets more comfy to listen from the sofa. Others stand and sip juice or cold beers with looks of curiosity, contentment, and a splash of gravity—for hearing a testimony of sorts invokes an earnest and sincere heart.

Feeling, as I was, in good company, I continue...

"Like I said, Ramesh's teaching was so effective, so brilliant! It got the job done. In my own case, it took about three years and three months from the time I met him on November 22, 2007, until awakening happened.

"Pretty much from the first day, those first few meetings with Ramesh, I had full intellectual understanding of his basic point that I cannot be the doer... That there is no individual doer, and that what happens has never been in anyone's individual control. 'Thy will be done.' That was easy for me to accept, for clearly, all I had to do was look at my own life, and the evidence was right there in front of me.

"It took about another year before that concept, if you will, deepened in understanding to the point where I could no longer refute even the smallest, tiniest happening. The ego was being rendered more and more helpless, weakening. Already with full intellectual understanding and then abiding acceptance of the truth-concept of non-doership (what Ramesh would describe as a *pointer*), my life became infinitely easier and simpler.

"Then, in May 2009, just a few months before Ramesh left the body, a curious thing happened. Up until that point, I'd jokingly considered Ramesh my *guru du jour*, not willing to pronounce him as my guru and not willing to pronounce myself as a disciple.

"Actually, that's not totally true—he was my teacher, and I was his student; that was clear. But I wasn't a *devotee*. The relationship was totally impersonal, and while there was reverence and affection from my side due to appreciation, it remained *jnana* – intellectual knowledge, a 'neck-up' realization.

"Then, while on a short visit back to the States for two weeks in springtime 2009, the oddest thing occurred. The jnana and understanding dropped into the heart and EXPLODED! Out of nowhere, I became Radha to Krishna, a drunken lover to the Truth as Beloved. It made no difference that I was ten thousand miles away from India: I knew I had to get back on that plane and return to Gamadia Road in Bombay to be with Ramesh and friends for his ninety-second birthday, to be celebrated on May 25.

"My friend Suresh had emailed me that, yes, Ramesh was planning on speaking that day, having been in the hospital and unwell off and on for months. I didn't care if it was one day or one hour to be in his divine presence! I booked my flight. Tears streamed down my cheeks as I wrote in my journal in the Delhi airport while awaiting my domestic connecting flight:

"The power of love will take you to the Moon and back!

"Bhakti had happened! I had fallen in love with the Truth, the satguru embodied in the form of Ramesh. From that May day on, Ramesh became much, much more to me than a simple instructor in non-duality, enlightenment, and liberation: he was my Advaita *Master*!

"Having had the power of love—bhakti—explode into the heart was the culmination of the jnana intellectual understanding becoming total. This *appeared* (though I have no way of knowing) to be a precursor of what happened next—the disappearance of the 'me,' the illusory separate self.

"In the early part of 2009, I had read a passage in one of Ramesh's books explaining that, *once a person has intellectual understanding of non-doership,* the best 'preparation' for enlightenment that anyone can 'do' is simply this: daily living. Nothing special, just normal daily activities! If it is God's will or cosmic law that a person wakes up, *it will happen*—and not a second before or after it is destined to happen. Daily life is the best 'preparation' for enlightenment.

"Because of the *intense* and *unwavering* faith in my Teacher, with total Trust—Surrender, if you will—that one line in the book inspired me and assured me I could *completely* and *totally* relax in every way. In fact, Ramesh used to say in his talks, 'The whole point is to relax!'

"So there it was, and life went on. About nine months after Ramesh died, I returned to the U.S. to finish my first book—a backpacker's adventure memoir about India—and to focus on other aspects of life for a while. Like I said, daily living.

"And then one day in early 2011—I think it was mid-February—just like that, nothing special, I woke up and realized *there was no one there*. It could have been morning, midday, puttering around the house, hanging laundry—daily living! Simply, there was no separate 'me,' no separate center of operations, so to speak. No one there. There was no Erin! Erin didn't exist!

"I kept looking for several days, to see if she (a 'me') may have temporarily disappeared or may have been merely hiding out somewhere in the mind. But she was nowhere to be found. I couldn't stop giggling whenever the thought (or rather, the *knowing*) arose that there was no Erin. Again, I would look, inquire within and try to find a 'me.' There was no one there.

"I giggled for about six months. It was hilarious. What a great cosmic joke! I soon found out that some of my friends didn't find it so amusing. I tried to tell them about it because I thought it was so funny, I had to share. I also was curious whether, if they looked, they would see it too. Was it the same for everybody? Wasn't it?

"After hardly anyone in my usual sphere got the joke, I shut up. I quickly learned that they were either concerned for my mental health, or they were truly confused by what I was trying to express.

"Slowly, it became just another happening, nothing special, and yet very, very special. The root of the ego had been cut, rendering it as useless as a burnt rope. Now I see what the sages mean when they say, 'There is no separate self.' Of course not, because there is no ME! There is the eternal I, and I am not separate from that. I AM THAT!

"Life has gone on—the pleasures come and go (which I totally enjoy, by the way; when surf's up, it's up!) and often pains, too. The body and psyche experience both completely, without the claiming by a conceptual 'me,' and without worry. In this way, life is much easier: even when circumstances are incredibly difficult or painful, there is simply enduring, or working, or experiencing whatever is arising in consciousness.

"I don't know if this seeing of *no one there, no me, no separate self* constitutes enlightenment, awakening, or realization—all big buzzwords these days. I can say that it brings a great deal of relief, happiness, amusement, and curiosity as to the unfolding of the play of Consciousness, and a simultaneous Nothingness about it.

There is nothing there.

I look, I look, and I look… and there is nothing.

Only experiencing.

Life happening."

> *Thy will be done.*
> *Ramesh's Grace.*
> *There is nowhere to go.*
> *There is nothing to do.*
> *In gratitude, I remain.*

The Guru Question
San Francisco
May 25, 2011

If a guru is necessary, a guru will happen.

For some people, it *is* necessary, because Existence brings it about—it happens. Who are we to judge whether it's some sort of "weakness" or "projection" (or the opposite—a requirement) to have a guru?

The appearance of a guru in human form may or may not happen in a spiritual seeker's lifetime of experience. I don't know why it happened in my case—destiny, I suppose. I do know that one month before events conspired to bring me to Mumbai to meet my teacher, I had prayed fervently: "God, if there is a teacher out there for me, *please*, I pray with all my heart, let me meet him or her."

You see, I was done. D-O-N-E with the seeking. I was tired of chasing tails. And I had lost hope that there could be a teacher out there for me—a sage so perfectly transparent and trustworthy that I could surrender in my heart and mind. It is said that is what it often takes before a person is ready to surrender. I thought it could never happen for me. (Heck, there's even a chapter in my *Bindi Girl* book about my guru allergy!)

It was Thanksgiving Day when I first entered the home of Ramesh Balsekar. In the two years I spent with him, I found him flawless, perfect in his transmission of Advaita; he was a Master.

They say when we meet our guru, it is perfection. That was my experience. My guru was perfect for me in every way. And therefore, it must also be perfect that Ramesh is no longer here in physical form, having left the body. I trust that there are reasons as to why I only got to be with my teacher for a short period. Perhaps it's because I need to be back in the West, and not tied to India. Perhaps two years were all I needed to be at the guru's feet. Perhaps the transmission, and our time together, were simply complete.

In one of our final private discussions a few months before he left the body, Ramesh asked me if I'd written yet about the teaching, the understanding of Advaita. I said, no, that it hadn't happened yet. Perhaps it is now arising—words to express the ineffable.

This is the first time in four years I haven't been able to be in Mumbai to celebrate the *jayanti* (birthday) of my beloved guru, born May 25, 1917. I can hardly express my infinite gratitude and celebration.

Thank you Ramesh-Guruji!

And thank you to grand-guru, Sri Nisargadatta Maharaj.

I'm so happy to be a part of this lineage.

To Be Awake
San Francisco
August 21, 2013

To be awake is to know with 100 percent certainty that there is only *now*. To have perfect faith in What Is, past, present and future. To no longer identify with the tiny "me," except as the barest slightness of ego that keeps the body-mind operational. To understand there is no central locus of the Self. To understand the perfection in all creation and happenings—that it's perfect, even when it appears not. And there is understanding that everything is happening according to God's will, cosmic law.

Daily life as an awake person functions pretty much the same as many people with highly evolved consciousness, except that the concept of a small self, a "me," has dissolved. There are more periods of simply sitting, staring off into space, waiting without expectation for the next moment to arise.

There is an absence of a "me" identifying with the pain or pleasure. If and when contraction arises, it is clearly seen as a witnessing of latent suffering, also known as *samskaras* or *vasanas* (latent karmic or habitual tendencies), and often experienced as transformation into pure consciousness through awareness. It is like Ramana Maharshi and many other sages have described: Once there is no longer identification with the ego, it is like a ceiling fan that continues to spin around for a while once the electric power has been turned off. The unwinding continues for as long as it continues. This is karma—apparent cause and effect—but there is no individual karma; everything is related to everything else for all time, all at once. Karma is not personal; it is not separate, except as an appearance.

The evolution of consciousness continues. The development of the human being continues. Learning and curiosity may continue. Life is "timepass" as the Indians call it—simply the passing of time. Spiritual, psychological, social, emotional, mental, and physical changes and growth likely continue. Pleasure and pain are felt more intensely, spontaneously, without filtering of "this should happen" or "this should not happen." There is a clear understanding, seeing, knowing that the ego is a drop of water in the Ocean of Being.

I continue to experience shaktipat as the Kundalini works Her way through and into my heart. These appear to be voltage shocks of grace that I've been experiencing since meeting my Teacher. I have no way of knowing when they will come or go or how long this will last. They usually, but not always, accompany an evolutionary leap in consciousness or a powerful spiritual experience. I've learned not to attach myself to the "heart shocks," but I must admit, I do enjoy them when they're afoot; they remind me of my beloved guru.

Post-awakening, I still experience the same biological urges. Desires arise, curiosities are sometimes carried through (for better or for worse!). Thoughts arise, but there truly is no thinker. Thinking—horizontal thinking (as Ramesh used to call identified thinking) that attaches itself to an illusory past or future does not occur. There is only vertical "now" thinking. Planning of the future or "dipping in" to the files/stories/information of the past occurs as a function of the working mind. The working mind/vertical thinking is the engaged mind, and not separate from What Is.

Siddhis (special powers like telepathy, seeing the future, etc.) come and go, but they are not clung to, pursued, nor are there fears of gaining or losing a power. Animal fears (involving food, shelter, clothing, safety) may arise, but anxiety practically does not exist. I may experience PTSD from traumas of the past, which can trigger the nervous system into an anxious, overly stimulated and shocked (fight, flight, freeze) state.

Other emotions continue, and even (gasp!) rage, anger, and fear arise. The shadow is seen for what it is. Preferences are completely accepted, and can change. Usually (but not always), a quieter life ensues. There is little to no worry or concern for "the future," which doesn't exist until it's in the now. There is complete acceptance of what comes as what comes; there is no longer frustration of the world being one way or another. Ambition changes: the old way of achieving drops away. There is no longer a need to prove oneself (since no separate self-locus exists). If goals or accomplishments or duties arise, they are dealt with as any normal person or according to the development/conditioning of the person at that point in time and space.

I was recently interviewed by author and non-dual teacher J. Stewart Dixon, who describes enlightenment as what is left after one has given up on the search for enlightenment—things are as they are, end of story.

At one point in our conversation, I told J. how much contraction and discomfort I feel when sitting before other non-dual teachers in the students' seats. It's like squishing oneself into too-small kid desks, like those in kindergarten, when you're really a post-doc. Something like that.

Post awakening, some keep going to teachers for a time because we're in the habit, we like the teacher or environment, or we like the sangha (community). Talking with an awake teacher is, well, normalizing and nice.

J. made the interesting point that he's been out of the closet a long time with regard to his enlightenment, and he is quite open about being awake. It's a relief. For some time now, he's been giving talks and coaching to folks seriously devoted to waking up. He told me that through his conversations with other "extra ordinary awake people," he has come to realize that the only thing left to do is to teach (speak, write, counsel, meaningfully entertain—whatever one's particular style).

It seems a natural course for awake folks to carry the message, to pass it on for no apparent reason other than that is what the Consciousness happens to express. Sitting in the contracted-suffering seat as a student when you've moved past the seeking stage can feel downright frustrating. It's like going back into suffering, unnecessarily. It still may happen as long as it happens. And there's no problem either way.

J. shared another interesting discovery he's made since interviewing folks for his book: how each "extra-ordinary" person that he's interviewed has his/her own individual bent on their awakening. That's my experience too. If I have a simple "twist" today, the easiest thing to say is, there's no *there* there. There's no "me"—it is like a concept, a soap bubble, just up and popped and dissolved one day. I can barely remember what it was like to believe in a separate, identified "me." It's empty.

Even though I did have a renowned Advaita Indian guru in my own unique "awakening" story (a truly lovely story!), I find it remarkable that I rarely use my own teacher's words verbatim. When I met him, the pointer to truth that impacted me deeply was the confirmation of non-doership. I already knew it, but needed a perfectly clear mirror before me in order to know that I knew. Such is the power of an awakened master and guru-disciple relationship. A guru is not necessary for awakening, unless it's necessary. Oh, the paradox of truth.

Each teacher has their own experience of waking up, and therefore what they say will be different. A student may or may not have the same experience. For instance, during the time I sat with Ramesh, he rarely discussed what it was like to be awake with no "me," leaving that to the individual to experience. He never scripted an awakening for me; he didn't tell me in advance that it would be like being without a central locus of operation—no CEO (Chief Erin Operator). That was for me to directly experience.

Ramesh's job was to make sure I had no further questions sprouting from the mind; when there was no confusion left, he made it clear that at that point, returning to daily living is the only thing left to do. The fact that awakening happened seventeen months *after* my Teacher died shows me that God (Life, Cosmic Law) has a sense of humor, and we can never know when it will happen. Once we have our basic questions answered, we can let go and live our daily lives. We trust that it will happen, when and if it is our destiny.

Tim(e) Will Tell
Harbin Hot Springs
September 9, 2013

I'm sitting in the Fireside Room in one of my favorite retreat spots, Harbin Hot Springs in Northern California. A visiting sadhu from Rishikesh, India, has just finished leading us in a Full Moon Vedic ceremony on this Monday, day of Shiva. It is his first time in the U.S., and he is ecstatic to be here. I am thrilled, too; India has finally come to visit *me*!

Now Baba is handing out *rakhis* (prayer ties) straight from the Motherland, India Herself. It is my turn to approach the front to receive the blessing. With my shawl covering my head, I sit cross-legged before Baba. It is my chance to break out my weak Hindi. "Mira nam Sapna hai!" *My name is Sapna!* I introduce myself with my India nickname, Sapna, a Hindi name that means "Dream." I use it for traveling purposes, and for fun. I smile as he prepares to bless me with the rakhi.

"Ahhh!" Baba's eyes sparkle with delight. "Sapna Devi! So good to see you, Mataji," he exclaims, using the most respectful term for a grown woman as respected mother. Baba mutters off a blessing in Sanskrit as he ties the red string 'round my right wrist, chanting all the while. He is smiling and giggling, a bubbling sound that suggests his glee at being spoken to in Hindi, unexpectedly.

Off to the side, I overhear a woman whisper to her friend, "Sapna...

that means dream." By the respectful way she wears a colorful shawl over her head and the ring in her nose, I guess that she, like me, has spent ample time in India.

I had been given the name Sapna seven years before, at the holy pilgrimage site of Pushkar, in Rajasthan. The full name had come to me one year later, in a dream.

SAPNA LILA DEVI
Dream Play Goddess

Though he'd never met me before this chance encounter at a California hot springs, Baba instinctively knew that part of my name was Devi. I'd been hesitant to use "devi" as it felt pretty bold to take on a title that means "Hindu mother goddess; supreme power in the universe; wife or embodiment of the female energy of Shiva." But now that the holy man had confirmed it, I could no longer refute it. Later, over chai in the common dining room, Baba says to me, "Sapna Devi, your devotion is beautiful."

Two days after the Full Moon Shiva puja, very early in the morning, I was writing in my journal by the side of the pool when suddenly and out of nowhere, my former boyfriend Tim appeared from thin air and grabbed me in a bear hug...

I was stunned—and thrilled! I'd heard hide nor hair from my former lover over the past six years as I'd kept a vow of no contact, "staying out of the picture," since we went our separate ways in India. Problem was, I had to obtain his permission to use his name in the book! What to do? I'd need to miraculously "run into" Tim in order to make contact. I had no idea how that would happen, especially since we lived in different parts of the country.

After we hugged hello, Tim explained he had just driven down from Oregon to camp at the springs, taking a little retreat for himself. He had felt pulled to visit at this time, for what reason he knew not, but being a completely connected mystic himself, he knew not to question a tug from the Divine. I marveled at how clear the energy was between us, how karma-free. It was such a wonderful feeling, knowing that staying out of each other's way over the last six years was exactly what was needed.

I cut straight to the chase, not knowing if Tim might evaporate as quickly as he appeared, "Do I have your permission to use your name in my book?" I asked him.

For the past several months, I'd wondered how to get in contact with Tim in order to ask his permission to use his name in my book. I didn't *want* to change his name to Fred or Joe or Mike. He was *Tim*! My partnER IN TIMe. But I couldn't email him, and like me, he wasn't on Facebook. I would be able to contact his family, but then I would be breaking my no-contact agreement. The only thing I had left to do was pray about it and wait.

"Sure, no problem. So long as you don't use my last name, right?" said Tim.

"Of course," I replied. "I might simply say you're from Indiana, though. To describe you."

Ten years my junior, Tim is a blond-haired, cornflower blue-eyed Indiana son. Yup, *India*-na! At first glance, his Midwestern good looks might prove distracting from noticing that he's also deeply spiritual and awake.

If Tim hadn't shown up in the movie of my life, likely I'd still be painfully wallowing in self-deprecation, suffering in the separation of "me" from the Source. This was the young man that helped me realize that awakening from the dream was possible, *here and now*. This was the man who led me to my spiritual master in India. How can you ever thank such a person enough?

Tim and I spent much of that Thursday—day of Jupiter and day of the guru—in the retreat center's garden, under the shady plum trees. We psychically checked under every rock and stone of history between us to see if even one tiny bit of karma still existed, if anything still needed to be ousted. Together we could find nothing, instead laughing at the comedy and perfection of existence. We reveled in the clarity of completion and the knowledge that we had done good work together and taught each other so much. It was a living, breathing example of what is possible when we set ourselves and the other free, over and over and over again. This is the miracle of detachment with love.

I left Tim expressing sheer gratitude for our "chance" meeting, along with an affirmation of his character. There was a reason I was with this man, and there was a reason I met him then and now.

As Ramesh used to say:

Never a need to worry.

Never a need to hurry.

We Are That
Northern California
September 27, 2013

The guru is no longer a separate person for me; the guru lives on, in my very heart. He has become me, and I am him. We Are That.

On this September 27 day of mahasamadhi, in eternal gratitude, I bow my head to the feet of my beloved teacher and guru, Ramesh Balsekar, a masterful sage and divine embodiment of truth.

And to the Goddess, Mother of the Universe, and to Shiva, the Is-ness that is All.

We are the Source, the Self.

We Are That.

In the state of self-realization,
all separation between God and the devotee disappears,
and the goal and the path become one.
All separation between the interconnected opposites disappears
and the split-mind is healed into its wholeness and holiness.
Indeed, worshipping and not worshipping,
action and non-action
lose their separateness and opposition
because all that happens
(the doing and the non-doing)

is spontaneous.
It is for this reason that the state of enlightenment
is beyond words and silence
and is described as indescribable,
and the Vedas at the end of an intense effort
confess their helplessness
in the words of Neti, Neti
(not this, not that).
~ Ramesh Balsekar

Epilogue:
Celebrating the Master Teacher

Royal Bombay Yacht Club, Mumbai
May 25, 2017

On this New Moon in the mutable air sign of Gemini, the Twins of Duality and Interconnected Opposites, I am halfway around the world back in the arms of my beloved Mother India.

It is auspicious that this New Moon falls on the Centenary birthday celebration of my Gemini teacher and Advaita master, Ramesh Balsekar, born on May 25, 1917. It has been my great honor to be of service at this gala event; I was invited by the organizers to be the Master of Ceremonies.

Facilitating the full-day ceremony for my Guruji was by far one of the biggest experiences of my life! Fellow teachers, students, lovers of our Guruji, family members, and bhakta devotees—all of us joined together at the Royal Bombay Yacht Club to celebrate this great man, who dropped his body on September 27, 2009. Ramesh's teaching and grace touched us to the core, transmitting the knowledge and understanding that surpasses suffering.

It was a day rich with eminent speakers, Sufi concerts, video premieres and book launches. All to celebrate our love for this great Teacher and the Understanding that, as Ramesh used to paraphrase the Buddha, "Events happen. Deeds are done. But there is no individual doer thereof."

A few snippets from my opening speech:

So how did I get here as the M.C. for all of us today? Perhaps a few words from Guruji himself might explain it perfectly:

"Consciousness has written the story, Consciousness has made this production, Consciousness is acting all the roles in this drama, and Consciousness is experiencing all the pleasure and the pain through the instruments which are human beings. What is really happening is ever since life began, life has always been the existence at the same time of interconnected opposites. Since the story has already been written—all that happens is that the movie is taking place and all we can do is witness it."

In other words, as Ramesh used to say, THE MOVIE IS IN THE CAN!

I don't usually speak much about the Teaching. Ramesh's transmission of Advaita lives so deep inside of my being, it is as if he is inside of me himself. I wouldn't be up here today if I wasn't asked, and perhaps I'm just the only one who was willing. As I said, it is for the deepest love of my Teacher. This love for the teaching is so far beyond the beyond that if I sit in presence with one of you and convey its enormity, I will simply cry and cry and cry, oceans upon oceans upon oceans of gratitude.

We all know our dear Ramesh was a big lover of jokes. And his biggest joke for me was when, about a year after Guruji passed away, I was back in California, hanging laundry on the clothesline one morning. From one moment to the next, I simply realized... there was a realization in this body-mind organism that there is NO ONE THERE. So simple, so subtle, it is an event hardly worth mentioning, and at the same time, it is the most incredible, important, and relieving thing that could have ever happened. In my own words, I describe it as the realization that there is no single central operating mechanism. As Ramesh would put it, there is the total apperception that there is no doer.

We all have our own way of putting it into words. That's one of the best parts of our beloved Teacher's transmissions: no one is parroting anything.

Just as Ramesh never parroted his own master, Sri Nisargadatta Maharaj. Our Guruji had his own style, and as he put it, his own concept of enlightenment, to which I say: it worked for me! And so many of us here today...

Acknowledgements

First, I thank my Teacher, Ramesh Balsekar. Without the appearance of this great sage in my story, I might still be suffering.

Next, I thank my Beloved, Keith Heller. I am beyond grateful to God for your presence in my life. Your support in getting me across the finish line with this book has been immense. Thank you for giving me all the space and quiet I require as a writer, contemplative, semi-hermit. I love you with all my heart.

Gratitude to Kelsey Conroy, Lynn Braz, Jill Merzon, Sasha Ronan, and Emma Nirmala Batchelor for their support, encouragement, and help with the manuscript. Sincere appreciation to Sharon Schanzer for the beautiful design, and to my initial reviewers, Mary Anker, Heidi Singfield, and Pat O'Hanrahan, for their insightful and useful feedback.

Thank you to my readers, students, and clients over the years. It has been a blessed journey. And to Tim, for showing up right on time.

Finally, a deep bow of love and gratitude for the land and people of India and the magical city of Mumbai.

Glossary

Adhitthana – strong spiritual determination
Advaita – non-duality
Agni – fire
Aloo – potato
Amritanubhava – experience of immortality
Ananda – peace, bliss
Anapana – awareness meditation, observing the breath
Aparigraha – non-hoarding, non-coveting, non-possession
Arhat – liberated person
Arunachala – holy mountain of Shiva in the form of fire
Asana – physical yoga practice
Ashram – place of spiritual retreat
Ayurveda – traditional Hindu system of natural medicine
Baba – renunciate or yogi; also refers to "father" as a form of respect
Baksheesh – tip or bribe
Bhagavan, Bhagwan – God or most holy revered person
Bhavan – spiritual teaching building
Bhakti – divine love
Bidi – tobacco leaf hand-rolled cigarette
Bindi – decorative or spiritual mark worn on the forehead of Indian women
Chalo – let's go, move on

Chandra – moon
Chapati – unleavened flatbread
Chit – consciousness
Dal – lentils
Das – servant
Darshan – holy presence
Devi – goddess
Dharma – eternal and inherent nature of reality; cosmic law
Dhuni – holy fire
Durga – wrathful goddess of strength
Ganesha – elephant-headed god; remover of obstacles
Ghat – steps leading to river or tank of water
Gita – song
Gobi – cauliflower
Gufa – cave
Guna – primal urges of nature
Gunātita – one who lives beyond primal urges
Guru – spiritual teacher
Haan – yes
Hanuman – monkey god of devotion and divine love
Hare – evocation of Krishna
Hari – evocation of Vishnu
Jata – matted hair; dreadlock
Jayanti – birthday
Jhula – bridge
Ji – term of respect
Jñana – knowledge
Kali – wrathful goddess of death and liberation
Karma – universal causal law
Karma Yoga – path of right action or service
Kundalini – life force energy coiled at the base of the spine
Lassi – sweet or savory drink made from yogurt or buttermilk
Lila – divine play, sport, game
Lungi – sarong-like wrap

Maa – mother
Maha – great
Mahabodhi – great awakening
Maharaj – great king
Maharshi – great sage or spiritual leader
Mahasamadhi – ultimate resting place or death of a realized sage
Mandir – temple
Maya – illusion
Moksha – ultimate freedom
Mouni – silence
Mudra – symbolic or ritual gesture or pose
Murti – idol
Nadi – river or stream
Nisarga – natural
Niyama – positive duties or observations
Paan – betel nut chew
Paani – water
Prana – life force, *chi*
Pranayama – breathing exercises of yoga
Puja – act of worship
Ram – avatar of Vishnu; synonymous with God
Raja Yoga – "king" or "royal" yogic path focusing on mind and body
Rajas – heat
Rishi – ancient sage of India
Rupee – currency of India
Sadhaka – spiritual practitioner
Sadhana – spiritual practice
Sadhu – holy men and women of India
Samadhi – intense peace or concentration usually achieved through meditation
Sapna – dream
Saraswati – goddess of knowledge, music, and the arts
Sat – truth
Satguru/Sadguru – true teacher

Satsang – spiritual gathering in truth
Sattva – quality of purity
Shakti – feminine force of the universe; power
Shaktipat – the transmission of spiritual energy from one individual to another
Shanti – peace
Shiva – god of creation and destruction
Siddhis – powers, abilities, attainments resulting from yogic practice
Sishya – disciple
Sita – wife of Rama; Hindu model of ideal feminine
Smasana – goddess of the cremation grounds
Sri – honorific term referring to respected holy person
Stupa – dome-shaped Buddhist shrine
Sutra – scripture
Tamas – quality of heaviness, dullness
Tandava – Shiva's dance of creation and destruction
Tantra – sacred practices or rituals
Tapas – heat, austerity, penance
Tapasya – inner discipline generating heat and intensity to awaken realization
Tilaka – a mark worn by a Hindu on the forehead
Upanishad – philosophical and religious texts of Hinduism
Vasistha – ancient and respected Vedic sage
Vedas – large body of religious texts originating in ancient India
Veena – ancient harp resembling a lute
Vibhuti – sacred ash
Vichara – self-inquiry
Wallah – man, often a trade worker
Yama – yogic social discipline, right action
Yogasana – the physical postures of yoga

References

Balsekar, Ramesh S. *The Experience of Immortality.* Chetana Books, 1997.

Balsekar, Ramesh S. and Mary Ciofalo, editor. *It So Happened That: The Unique Teaching of Ramesh S. Balsekar with Stories and Anecdotes.* Zen Publications, 2000.

Balsekar, Ramesh S. *Peace and Harmony in Daily Living: Facing Life Moment to Moment.* Yogi Impressions, 2016.

Hixon, Lex. *Great Swan: Meetings with Ramakrishna.* Larson Publications, 1997.

Maharaj, Sri Nisargadatta and Maurice Frydman, translator. *I Am That: Talks with Sri Nisargadatta Maharaj.* Chetana Publications, 1973

Maharshi, Sri Ramana and David Godman, editor. *Be As You Are: The Teachings of Sri Ramana Maharshi.* Sri Ramanasramam, 1985.

Osborne, Arthur. *Ramana Maharshi and the Path of Self-Knowledge.* Sri Ramanasramam, 1997.

Reese, Erin. *The Adventures of Bindi Girl: Diving Deep Into the Heart of India.* Travel and Soul Media, 2012.

Yogananda, Paramahansa. *Autobiography of a Yogi.* Philosophical Library, 1946.

About the Author

Erin Reese, M.S., is a teacher in the Advaita lineage of Ramesh Balsekar and Sri Nisargadatta Maharaj. She is also an intuitive consultant worldwide. Erin lives in the High Sierra of Northern California with her Beloved, Keith.

For more information, visit erinreese.com.

Made in the USA
Columbia, SC
10 June 2021

39653501R00136